THE POCKET IDIOT'S GUIDE TO

Poker Tells

*by Bobbi Dempsey
and Andy Bloch*

ALPHA

A member of Penguin Group (USA) Inc.

ALPHA BOOKS

Published by the Penguin Group

Penguin Group (USA) Inc., 375 Hudson Street, New York, New York 10014, U.S.A.

Penguin Group (Canada), 10 Alcorn Avenue, Toronto, Ontario, Canada M4V 3B2 (a division of Pearson Penguin Canada Inc.)

Penguin Books Ltd, 80 Strand, London WC2R 0RL, England

Penguin Ireland, 25 St Stephen's Green, Dublin 2, Ireland (a division of Penguin Books Ltd)

Penguin Group (Australia), 250 Camberwell Road, Camberwell, Victoria 3124, Australia (a division of Pearson Australia Group Pty Ltd)

Penguin Books India Pvt Ltd, 11 Community Centre, Panchsheel Park, New Delhi—110 017, India

Penguin Group (NZ), cnr Airborne and Rosedale Roads, Albany, Auckland 1310, New Zealand (a division of Pearson New Zealand Ltd)

Penguin Books (South Africa) (Pty) Ltd, 24 Sturdee Avenue, Rosebank, Johannesburg 2196, South Africa

Penguin Books Ltd, Registered Offices: 80 Strand, London WC2R 0RL, England

Copyright © 2005 by Bobbi Dempsey

All rights reserved. No part of this book shall be reproduced, stored in a retrieval system, or transmitted by any means, electronic, mechanical, photocopying, recording, or otherwise, without written permission from the publisher. No patent liability is assumed with respect to the use of the information contained herein. Although every precaution has been taken in the preparation of this book, the publisher and authors assume no responsibility for errors or omissions. Neither is any liability assumed for damages resulting from the use of information contained herein. For information, address Alpha Books, 800 East 96th Street, Indianapolis, IN 46240.

THE POCKET IDIOT'S GUIDE TO and Design are trademarks of Penguin Group (USA) Inc.

International Standard Book Number: 978-1-59257-454-4
Library of Congress Catalog Card Number: 2005933827

09 08   8 7 6 5 4 3

Interpretation of the printing code: The rightmost number of the first series of numbers is the year of the book's printing; the rightmost number of the second series of numbers is the number of the book's printing. For example, a printing code of 05-1 shows that the first printing occurred in 2005.

Printed in the United States of America

Note: This publication contains the opinions and ideas of its authors. It is intended to provide helpful and informative material on the subject matter covered. It is sold with the understanding that the authors and publisher are not engaged in rendering professional services in the book. If the reader requires personal assistance or advice, a competent professional should be consulted.

The authors and publisher specifically disclaim any responsibility for any liability, loss, or risk, personal or otherwise, which is incurred as a consequence, directly or indirectly, of the use and application of any of the contents of this book.

Most Alpha books are available at special quantity discounts for bulk purchases for sales promotions, premiums, fund-raising, or educational use. Special books, or book excerpts, can also be created to fit specific needs.

For details, write: Special Markets, Alpha Books, 375 Hudson Street, New York, NY 10014.

To Bulldog—we hit the jackpot with an ace of a friend like you. You were gone too soon, but will never be forgotten.

Contents

Introduction

Some people believe that winning at poker is all about luck. Those are usually the people who end up losing their shirts at the casino. We take a more practical approach. Sure, we all know there's an element of chance involved with every game. But there's also a lot of skill and strategy involved. That's why lots of practice and study can improve your skills as a player. It's also why you need every strategic advantage you can get.

Good intuition and sharp observational skills are essential tools at the poker table. In order to outsmart and outplay your opponents, you need to be able to read them correctly, and quickly. How? By watching for little clues and signals they're giving off without even being aware of it.

These little gestures, movements, or sounds are called tells, and they can give you a wealth of information about the other players at the table. By learning how to spot tells, you can play the game from a much better strategic standpoint. You can decide when to fold, or when your opponent is just trying to convince you to fold.

No matter what your skill level as a poker player, you can benefit from improving your ability to spot tells. As co-author Andy can attest, even the most experienced poker players sometimes miss—or misread—tells. And they sometimes slip up and give off a few tells, too. So there are plenty of opportunities for an eagle-eyed player to spot these clues. Hopefully, after reading this book, that lucky player will be you. Who knows—maybe one day soon, you'll find yourself sitting at a high-stakes tournament right along with Andy and the other pros. If so, he'll be sure to be on his toes—because he knows you'll be keeping a close watch for any tells.

As you read this book, you'll find little extra tidbits of information that we hope will be like small "golden nuggets" of poker wisdom for you. They are:

Lucky Lingo

Important poker terms and phrases you need to know.

Tilt

Warnings to help you avoid poker table pitfalls.

Help Card

Tips, advice, and useful information.

Bet You Didn't Know

Interesting or surprising poker facts.

Acknowledgments

Bobbi Dempsey would like to thank, first and foremost, her co-author Andy, whose guidance and input were invaluable, and Edward Carpenter, who provided research assistance. Then there are John, Nick, Brandon, and Jack. Last, her favorite celebrity poker players, Ben Affleck and Sara Rue—who, she is sure, will be inviting her over to join them in a poker game any day now.

Andy Bloch says, "One doesn't become a skillful poker player just by learning the rules and playing with a deck of cards. I owe most of my poker education to a large and diverse group of people. First, to the friendly dealers, floorpeople, and players (some of them not so friendly) at Foxwoods—where I got my start playing poker in casinos—and casinos around the world. Second, to those who posted at rec.gambling in the early 1990s, the players at the Boston-area WNPG, and the "Roolerz." To name just a few: Steve Brecher, Rick Charles, Chris Ferguson, Patri Friedman, Jim Geary, Lee Jones, Paul Phillips, Paul Pudaite, the Scheinbergs, Peter Secor, Bill Seymour, Tom Sims (the human hole-card cam), Marty Stillings, Bill Turner, Chuck Weinstock, and Michael Zimmers. To the MIT blackjack team, for giving me the primary source of income to quit my job and my start as a full-time professional gambler. And, more recently, to Team Full Tilt Poker, including: Howard Lederer, Phil Ivey, Chris Ferguson, John Juanda, Jennifer Harman, Phil Gordon, Erick Lindgren, Erik Seidel, Clonie Gowen, and the 20 or so other pros that also play on and represent the site.

I owe thanks to my family and friends not mentioned above, including Nadine, Joanne, Jon, Binyamin, Yoel, Shani, Margot, Joe Gersten, Rafe Furst, Richard Brodie, Jeff Shulman, James Arrowood, Ray Bitar, Jason Newitt, Annie Duke, to someone really important whom I am forgetting, to Suzie Lederer, for introducing me to my fiancé, and, of course, to my fiancé Jen.

Finally, I owe the greatest thanks to my parents who brought me up to be prepared for success in any endeavor, who always encouraged me to seek out my own happiness along the way, and whom I hope I can make proud with whatever I can eventually accomplish through the fame and fortune that has come to me through poker."

Trademarks

All terms mentioned in this book that are known to be or are suspected of being trademarks or service marks have been appropriately capitalized. Alpha Books and Penguin Group (USA) Inc. cannot attest to the accuracy of this information. Use of a term in this book should not be regarded as affecting the validity of any trademark or service mark.

Chapter 1

The Basics

In This Chapter

- The allure of poker
- Tells: defined
- Why tells are important
- The different kinds of tells

People often say that the eyes reveal the soul of a person. People may also say that tells reveal the poker player. Poker is a psychological game. This book shows you how to read your opponent's facial expressions and body language, and helps you win the psychological battles that are at the heart of poker.

This chapter starts with an explanation of why so many people play poker. Then we define tells and explain why they are important to your strategy of play.

Why Play Poker?

Of all the ways you could spend your time—and possibly a great deal of money—why play poker? Because, in the words of a wise Vegas dealer, "Son, in the history of the world, no one's ever dealt a losing game of poker ...."

Think about it. In a game like roulette, hours can pass with no lucky winners. But with poker, every time the cards are dealt, someone wins. The only question is, of all the hopeful gamblers at the table, who's it going to be?

Poker is the greatest gambling experience in the world because, unlike craps, roulette, blackjack, or baccarat, it is a game of skill, not merely chance. Granted, there *is* a large measure of luck and chance built into poker. The game wouldn't be a gamble without it.

Although there's no way to predict what cards you will get, there is always a winning strategy for every hand, in every situation. A player with a hand of 2-3 can beat a pair of Aces without breaking a sweat. We've seen it happen a hundred times.

But we suspect that we're preaching to the choir here. If you're reading this book, we assume that you've already developed a love of the game. You've probably spent many hours at various poker tables—or camped in front of your computer, if you're an online fan. Odds are, you've already mastered the basics of good poker play. Now you're looking for a way to bring your skills to the next level. This is where we can help.

A Few Assumptions

Yes, we know the old saying about never assuming anything, but we're going to do it anyway. In this book, we assume that you already know the basics of poker. So we won't waste time going over the general stuff, such as the terminology of poker, the rankings of the hands, some odds of drawing particular hands, the importance of seating positions, how to read the table, and basic betting strategy.

For the sake of consistency, when discussing specific hands, we assume we're playing Texas Hold'Em, the most common casino version of poker. Still, you can apply the lessons of this book to *any* poker game. From a stud game played around the kitchen table with friends to Omaha Hi-Lo in Las Vegas, the strategies in this book will help you to read your opponents tells, giving you better odds of being the one to win.

Thinking Like a Warrior

We mentioned earlier that the heart of poker is psychological warfare, so a quote from one of the greatest military minds of all time, the ancient Chinese philosopher Sun Tzu, seems appropriate. In his famous work *The Art of War*, Sun Tzu said, "When you are ignorant of the enemy but know yourself, your chances of winning or losing are equal."

That is the approach many people take when they play poker. They know the right ways to bet their cards, but they don't "know" their opponents. Remember, in poker, you aren't just playing the hand you were dealt; you're playing against human opponents. And, humans can give small clues, which you can use to decide whether to check, bet, or fold.

This brings us to the meat of this book; you can use those small signals, known as "tells," to give you an edge over your less-observant opponents.

What Are Tells?

Most people have a strong unconscious impulse to behave in a certain way if they have either really strong cards, or really weak ones. Humans are creatures of habit. Veteran poker player Edward H. Carpenter shares an example of a *tell* he used to show when he first started playing poker: "If I had very strong cards, for example, A-A with a 6-A-J on the flop, I would play conservatively; checking, calling, and trying to let someone else build the pot for me, waiting until the last couple of rounds of betting, and employing a check-raise to milk a few more dollars out of my opponents. A good strategy, but the only problem was that it's not terribly exciting. So I would start shuffling chips or building little castles to pass the time. Looking back, I have to laugh, because this was an incredibly obvious tell for anyone who was paying attention, and a smart player who saw me start to build a castle of chips right after the flop would be wise to fold against me."

Lucky Lingo

A **tell** is any distinctive action made by an opponent that gives others a clue as to the strength or weakness of his or her hand.

Learning how to read other players' tells can be a huge asset in poker. But remember, you also have to guard against your *own* natural tendency to behave in predictable, observable manners.

Tilt

Keep in mind that some people may deliberately use false tells to confuse observant opponents. In fact, as you develop your poker game, this is a strategy you might use to get one up on the opposition.

Types of Tells

We can break down tells into several categories. We discuss each type in greater detail in the following chapters. For now, we categorize them as physical tells, physiological tells, pattern tells, and speed tells.

A physical tell is any visible, conscious action that a player makes using body language, hands, chips, food, cards, and so on. Physical tells include verbalizations such as sighs, grunts, and talking.

A physiological tell is similar to a physical tell, but is more closely related to unconscious bodily functions, such as increases in the rate of breathing and nervous twitching.

Pattern tells relate to a gambler's betting sequence. You need to invest some time—and use your observational skills—to detect this kind of tell. Eventually you may pick up on the fact that a player behaves a certain way when he or she has a specific kind of hand.

Speed tells are common in online poker, but occur at live games as well. Someone might take a long time to make his or her action, seemingly hesitant as to whether to call or fold. This is commonly a sign of a player with a strong hand attempting to appear weak, causing players with weak cards to stay in the hand longer and build the pot.

Is It Cheating?

Having the ability to read other players' tells can give you a huge advantage at the poker table. Some might wonder if that's an unfair advantage. People frequently ask us whether reading tells is considered cheating, and the answer is a definite "No!"

In fact, the use of tells to "read" your opponents is an integral part of the game of poker, and has been throughout the history of the game. It's exactly what Kenny Rogers was talking about when he said, "Son, I've made a life outta reading people's faces ...." So don't feel as if you are doing anything underhanded if you hone your ability to read tells and work on detecting and eliminating your own tells.

HELP **Help Card**

After you have mastered the basics, you might deceive your opponents by using false tells of your own to goad them into betting or to convince them to fold early.

You know the old saying "All's fair in love and war"? Well, we think it might be amended to say "All's fair in love, war, and poker"!

Where to Use Tells

How much use you will get out of learning to read tells largely depends on where and how you play poker. You won't always need—or want— to use tells. Some important factors will be the skill level of your opponents, and whether you've had a chance to observe them in play and watch their patterns and behavior.

The Venue Matters

It takes a while to figure out what tells a player reveals, and, remember, your average poker game has 8 to 10 people in it. So, if you play for one weekend in Atlantic City at a table where a lot of people are coming and going throughout the game, you might not have time to key in to more than a few obvious tells from certain players.

On the other hand, if you play in a weekly card game in your neighborhood where you see the same faces again and again, you can probably bene-fit a lot from reading tells.

Online Gambling

Online gambling was supposed to spell the end of reading tells, but, in fact, it has made learning your opponents' habits easier. If you play regularly on a particular poker site—especially if you focus on a certain category of games, such as 20-40 Texas Hold'Em—you'll see the same *handles* (user names) appearing over and over again. You can easily make a list on paper of repetitive traits that you notice, something that would be strongly discouraged at a live game.

  Lucky Lingo

A **handle** is a nickname or user name employed by a player online.

Low Limit or High Stakes?

It might seem like a low-limit game would be a good place to start learning to read tells, but, in fact, it's one of the worst and hardest. The people who play in these games are usually beginners or players who can't make it in higher-limit games. These players characteristically play a loose or very random game; they probably do not read the board very well, but yet they win against more experienced players because the smart money may read the board and fold early against a person with weak cards who raises. Or if the new player doesn't know any better, he or she may hold on to weak cards through a series of strong raises and re-raises, and may finally catch a lucky card on the river to complete a small straight, flush, or three-of-a-kind, beating hands that could play strong through the whole game. Similarly, at the highest levels of poker, the caliber of the players is such that it's easy to misread your opposition. Sometimes, this is a result of an opponent who deliberately plays a style that doesn't make sense to the average person. For example, a high-caliber player might go all in on a marginal hand at a bad time. Most people, even experts, fold against that kind of play, unless they hold really strong cards.

Fortunately, reading tells is the most useful at the level of mid-money range games, where the largest number of people will play seriously, such as 15-30, 20-40, and 30-60 Texas Hold'Em. Here, the value of the antes weeds out most beginners and those gamblers who are too poor or too inconsistent in their play to survive for more than a few hands.

Bet You Didn't Know

Reading tells may be most important in televised championship poker tournaments. Co-author Andy has noticed that many players give off more tells in events such as the $10,000 buy in World Series of Poker championship, because they are playing for so much more money than they ever have before, with the added pressure of television. Plus, many of the entrants win their way in for a fraction of the buy in and have little experience playing in live tournaments.

Consistency Is Key

If you play consistently in a particular venue with the same group of people, whether it's online, in a local Indian casino, or in a big-name casino in Las Vegas, New Orleans, or Atlantic City, you are going to start seeing familiar faces pretty quickly. That's important, because you need to play against someone for a while to pick up on his or her tells.

Your opponents are probably at your level of card play; this forces you to play smart and to use your ability to read people to win.

You need to pay attention to every hand, whether you are in it or not. In fact, sometimes it's easiest to learn when you're out of a hand; you can concentrate on reading the board and the other players. Try to gauge which player will win the hand. How early can you tell?

Tilt

Evaluate your own play. Look at your own play from your opponents' perspective, to make sure that you won't be too predictable. Try to keep it as varied as possible without being reckless. As an example, before the flop, do you always re-raise with A-A or K-K and little else? Try just calling a raise once in a while with them, and re-raise occasionally with other hands. Otherwise, a sharp opponent will figure out after a few hours that any time you re-raise before the flop, you're holding a strong pair—and when you don't, you're not.

Finally, take notes on every player you consistently meet. You won't be able to do this at the table, so use your head. Keep a small notepad in your pocket and jot down key tells when you take a break to use the bathroom or stretch your legs. This is completely legitimate and will help you remember a given player's tells for the next time you run into him or her.

The Least You Need to Know

- ◆ Poker is a unique form of chance. Any player can win any given game with virtually any hand.

- ◆ Learning how to read tells is a priceless skill for any poker player.

- ◆ People exhibit several different types of tells: physical, physiological, pattern, and speed tells.

- ◆ While paying attention to other players' tells, do not exhibit tells of your own.

Chapter 2

Player Personalities

In This Chapter

- Why typecasting players pays off
- Fish, rock, or something else?
- The best strategy for beating each personality

When it comes to poker, most people have a specific style of play and tend to stick to this approach for most, if not all, of their games. Players with certain styles tend to follow predictable patterns and exhibit specific tells. By sizing up an opponent's poker personality, you can often make a good guess about what they will do in a certain situation.

Pinpointing the Personality

Just like you can easily categorize certain actors and actresses by what sort of movies they are likely to play in, so can you categorize many card players by what hands they will play and how they will play them.

For example, it would not surprise anyone to hear that Jim Carrey is starring in a new comedy. But it would be a little odd to see Anthony Hopkins playing in a similar role. In every aspect of reading your poker opponents, you can try to start with the simplest things first and find some parallel in other aspects of life to help "make sense" of what you see at the card table. Hence, you can compare poker to acting, which you can use to "typecast" your opponents at the table.

Now, assuming that you don't have X-ray vision, how is it possible to tell what cards another player holds? Well, let's say the person in question has been sitting across from you for an hour and a half, and besides her blinds, she's only been in on three hands. She's folded all but one of the blinds after the flop, and of the four hands she's played, she has won three of them with Q-Q, A-K, and K-K. She had one bad beat where her J-J played with 10-J-2 on the flop, 4 on the turn, and a 10 on the river gave her opponent 10s over Jacks.

Now she has just anted; what is she holding?

You could bet money that she is holding a pair of Jacks or better. So if you don't have something stronger, you're probably going to fold your hand. Because remember, you'd prefer to win, not to gamble; and regardless of what anyone else at the table may be holding, if you're not holding some high face cards of your own, preferable Q-Q or better, then you're probably not going to beat this woman without relying on luck and the cards. You'd rather save your money, right?

This is just one example of using your natural powers of observation to read an opposing player and determine with a fair degree of accuracy what their hole cards are.

Help Card _____

Sometimes it's enough just to know that you *don't* know what someone's holding. That in and of itself may be enough to decide whether to raise, call, or fold.

The Five Player Varieties

Poker players can be categorized by two characteristics: aggressiveness and card strength. Using those two factors, we come up with five major types of players.

By aggressiveness, we mean a player's willingness to take more risks and challenge other players more often. Card strength refers to the strength and their hand, and the odds that it will be a winning hand.

The first variety is the "fish," who will call with almost any cards and is obviously a poor player. The second variety is the "weak" player who will play less often, and with better cards, but will generally fold in the face of pressure unless he or she's got a great hand.

Third, there's the "loose aggressive" player who plays very hard and fast. Like the fish, he will play almost anything, but, unlike the first two types, he will play these cards strongly—betting, raising, re-raising. He will frequently win against weaker players just due to forceful play. However, the "loose aggressive" player will have difficulty against the "tight aggressive" player—this is the fourth category of player, and where you want to play. The tight aggressive player waits for good cards, but, unlike the weak player, doesn't fold under pressure. Rather, he or she will play the hand through, and won't be put off by the bluffing of any "loose aggressive" players in the hand.

Finally, the fifth variety is the other extreme. The "rock" is the super-conservative player who will wait hours to get an AA or KK, and when he or she does, will play it all the way to the river. These players will tend to win their pots, but the pots won't be big, because anyone who is paying attention will get out of the hand early, as it's so obvious what the "rock" is holding.

Now let's talk about each of these types of players in more detail to determine how you can most quickly detect and take advantage of their playing styles.

The Fish

The fish is the loose, passive player, often referred to as the "calling station" because he rarely folds and will call with almost anything. The fish can be a frustrating opponent.

From our perspective, the fish has both good and bad characteristics. The good thing is that he is a pretty common character, and he loses a lot of money, because he exhibits the worst possible playing style.

The bad thing is that because this style of play is exactly the opposite of what he should do, and hence the opposite of what rational, educated players expect, it makes "reading" him difficult to do. So, how do you deal with a player of this type?

It's simple; don't try too hard to read what his hand is. Instead, make note of his behavior and ID him as a fish as quickly as possible. This behavior includes the following:

- ◆ He stays in on almost every hand.
- ◆ He tends to check or call instead of raising.

- He will go to the river every time.
- His wins reflect luck (for instance, his hole cards are 9-2, with 3-K-Q-2-2 on the board) versus skill.

Once you have identified this player as a fish, you should generally ignore him and focus on playing your cards and reading more dangerous players at the table.

The only exception to this will be if he raises. Because the fish is a passive player, he may call a lot but won't tend to raise without good cards. The fish is not a sophisticated-enough player to bluff, so you should tend to respect his raises, especially if they occur late in the hand. Remember the previous example of a board showing 3-K-Q-2-2; even if you're holding a strong hand like K-Q, you might fold against a fish's raise on the river.

Tilt

Knowing when to fold, especially when to fold "good" cards, is one of the hardest and most important lessons to learn in poker. No matter how good your cards are, if you're not fairly certain that they're winning cards, you have to be able to let them go and save your chips for a better hand.

The other case when a fish may raise is before the flop with strong cards such as AA, KK, and so on. Again, this will help you decide whether to play the cards you're holding. A drawing hand like J-10 (suited) will probably play well here, while otherwise fairly strong hole cards like A-K or 10-10 might not.

The Weak Player

The weak player is more of a rare breed than the fish. She might have generally good poker skills, but merely lack the confidence to capitalize on her opportunities. Sometimes this is the result of moving up to a higher limit game; an otherwise good player may become too focused on the relatively small size of her bankroll and hence be prone to the weak play (folding too early and too often with decent cards), which is indicative of the weak player.

Another contributing factor to weak play is that these players may be overly analytical and try to play some sort of system, such as, "If my hole cards are JJ, I will ante; if I get another J on the flop, I will raise; if not, I will call unless there is a re-raise and then I will fold."

This kind of play doesn't hold up well because it doesn't take into account the other types of players at the table and what hands they are likely to have. It doesn't take into account tells or table position or any number of other variables. Poker is part science and part art, and the weak player only knows the science. She can probably tell you exactly what the probability is of seeing a particular card on the turn, but she lacks the art of knowing that regardless of what that card is, the two other players in the hand are both loose aggressives and are very likely holding trash hands. And that her Q-10 along with the board's 2-9-10 is probably going to hold up. So she will probably get pushed out of this pot, and one of the aggressives will win with a small pair or high card or maybe will get lucky and improve on the turn or the river. But it won't matter, because she will have mucked another decent hand.

A weak player can be identified as follows:

- ◆ Doesn't play a lot of hands.
- ◆ Has a high percentage of early folds against stiff betting on hands she does play.
- ◆ When she wins, it is with the nuts—the only thing she's confident to play through with.

Once you've picked these players out, here's how to play them. You won't have to pay too much attention to them because they won't be in a lot of hands. However, if they are, be aware that they have pretty good hands, probably something in the top two or three tiers of poker hands. (If this doesn't make sense, grab a good book on poker theory, try *The Complete Idiot's Guide to Gambling Like a Pro* or *The Pocket Idiot's Guide to Texas Hold 'Em*.)

Also, although you know their hands are going to be good, they won't necessarily be the best, and they are very susceptible to bluffing, especially if the board shows something scary like a potential flush or full house. Remember, unlike the fish, these players are probably technically proficient and actually do read the board. So, if you are holding the nuts, play this type of opponent very slowly and gently. And if you're not, bluff big and scare them out of the pot.

The Loose Aggressive Player

More common than the weak player is the loose aggressive player. You will see this type of gambler a lot, almost as frequently as the fish. In fact, the big difference between the two is that while both play the same hands, the loose aggressive plays them hard and fast—often winning by driving smarter and more cautious players out of the game. If this player goes all the way to the river, he's got just as good a chance as the fish to pick something up by blind luck, but by then there are probably fewer players in the hand, so he has a better chance of winning out.

Like all player types, there are good and bad things about this type of player. You can make a lot of money from him, because typically the pots will be large in a game with one or more loose aggressive players. The problem is that due to his habit of raising and re-raising, if you do hit a bad beat against this player, it's going to be costly.

Here are characteristics of the loose aggressive player:

- Plays a lot of hands
- Raises frequently, too frequently ...
- Has many wins before the river; for instance, all other players fold after a high bet or re-raise.
- Showdowns indicate fewer premium cards, more lucky draws for the win.

Help Card

You can profile loose aggressives right away sometimes; a young male who bets really quickly and tends to slam the chips down is almost certainly going to turn out to be a loose aggressive.

When playing against a loose aggressive player, keep the following things in mind:

- Just because he is raising doesn't mean he has premium cards. Put your mind into playing your hand, the board, and other more dangerous players.
- Let him do the work of raising; it will save you money on those occasions when he really *does* have good cards. Call a lot against the loose aggressive.

The inherent weakness of the loose aggressive player is that he is betting too high on too many hands. So, you should do well against this type of player by playing a higher number of hands yourself—not every hand (that would make you just as bad as the loose aggressive) but a hand that you would probably fold against a more conservative player, such as Q-10 with a K-5-10 flop. Even though you've only got middle pair here, you know that the loose player could easily have a hand full of nothing; and you have two outs to pick up a second pair or a set. This makes it a much better pot to stay in than if you were faced with a tight aggressive player, or a rock.

The Tight Aggressive Player

The tight aggressive player is someone like yourself; or rather, like you should be. He picks his pots to play, not just based on his starting hand or what's showing on the board, but also on the other players in the hand, and their reading of tells suggesting what hole cards those players have.

If you plotted out the five poker personalities on a chart, you'd see that the tight aggressive player sits dead center on aggressiveness versus card strength. From this central position, he controls all the other players at the table. He is patient enough to wait for strong cards, and has enough finesse to play them softly if the situation dictates. He's also confident enough to withstand raises from players he knows are loose, and dominant enough to play strong and force weak players out of pots.

This player does not appear to play very many hands. When he does, he tends to win. And he doesn't always win by maniacal raises and re-raises. Sometimes he does; sometimes he may check or call all the way through and win a big pot with a nut hand, a big pot that some loose aggressive players raised up for him.

Sometimes he folds cards that he had been playing strongly. Of all the players in the game, this is the worst to play against, and also where tells are going to make you the most money. Fortunately, this type of player is rarer than the other four we're discussing.

Signs of a tight aggressive player include these:

+ Not playing many hands.
+ Winning a high percentage of hands played.
+ Calm, collected behavior whether winning or losing a hand.
+ Winning unexpectedly; for example, he caught a nut flush on the turn but called conservatively into a loose aggressive player, and re-raised on the river.

How do you beat the tight aggressive? By only playing solid hands when they are in the pot, and by developing your ability to read tells. Be prepared to break even against these players; you don't have to always win against them, just so long as you don't always lose to them. Try to minimize your losses by knowing when to fold a hand, even a good one, against a strong player.

The Rock

Remember our friend the fish? Well, the rock is the other end of the spectrum. While the fish bites at anything, the rock won't play with anything but premium cards.

She's quite happy to sit there smiling and throwing away hand after hand before the flop. Sipping a drink and scrutinizing the other players, or maybe staring off into space when she's out of a hand.

When the rock does ante up for a hand, it is only because she holds AA, KK, QQ .... This makes the rock the easiest read in the game; unlike the fish, where you have no idea what they have, with the rock, you can narrow it down to about four or five possible hands.

At a table with enough fish or loose players who aren't paying attention to the blatant signal that this player is holding big cards, the rock will win. But you can win from the rock by stealing blinds from him and bluffing him whenever he shows the first sign of weakness after the flop, while staying out of his way whenever he shows strength.

Bet You Didn't Know

It's a common fallacy that you can't beat a table full of bad players by playing tight like a rock. You can, and you will, if you have the fortitude and bankroll to withstand the large swings. But if you are a good player, you can do better by playing a little looser than the rock—but with even greater swings.

The Least You Need to Know

- By figuring out an opponent's player personality, you can often anticipate what he or she will do in certain situations.

- The fish is considered the least dangerous player, so you should focus your energy on stronger players in the game.

- A weak player is generally proficient at the game, but is susceptible to bluffing.

- The loose aggressive player tends to be a fast and furious type of player, one who will drive more cautious types out of the game.

- The tight aggressive is a cautious, patient and confident player who can be a challenge to beat.

Chapter 3

Tells of Novice Players

In This Chapter

- Quick ways to spot pros
- Why knowing who's a novice is important
- The common signs of a novice

It probably goes without saying that inexperienced players tend to give off the most—and most obvious—tells. Poker pros are savvy enough to read opponents' tells, and avoid giving tells of their own. In this chapter, we cover some basic tells that you commonly see when you play with inexperienced opponents.

The Basics of Novice Tells

In the movie *Rounders*, Matt Damon's character has a great line—the gist of it says that if you can't spot the sucker at a table within the first half-hour, it's probably you. It's a humorous way to put it, but it's also pretty accurate.

It's also a fitting way to start off on this topic, which discusses how to spot and read the tells of novice players.

> ### Bet You Didn't Know
>
> *Rounders* is a staple of every poker fan's movie collection. This 1998 film featured Matt Damon as a compulsive gambler who loses his law school tuition—and pretty much everything else he owns—in a high stakes game of poker. He gives up gambling, until he is forced back into it to help his friend win money to repay a debt to a mobster. If you have never seen the movie, we would definitely recommend it.

Why It's Important to Read Tells

Why is it so important for an up-and-coming poker pro to be able to read tells of novice players? Well, in a perfect world, it would be ideal if every poker player had a sign identifying him as a novice or expert. Unfortunately, that doesn't happen in the real world. Therefore, it's important for you to learn how to quickly decipher beginners from experts. In order to do this, it's generally wise to observe a table for a while before jumping in to play.

Of course, it won't be as easy as our little sample scenario. Anyone with enough cash can typically play at any casino table. And novice players won't be identified by helpful place cards or flashing neon signs above their heads.

Sample Scenarios

If you learn to quickly differentiate the novices from the stronger players, you can give yourself an advantage, and decide whether and how to play so-so hands.

Let's say you play at a 20-40 table in Vegas. After you observe the players in action, you determine that five of them seem new to the game. One guy is clearly a better player than you, and the remaining players are roughly at the same skill level as you. Right off the bat, this table is a good one for you, because at least half the players are less skilled than you.

Now let's see what happens in two hypothetical scenarios.

In the first scenario, you've been dealt 7-8. You are acting last, and so far, three players have folded, and the rest have anted up to see the flop. Now, in this case, the players who folded were all guys you pegged as novices, which means that the four strongest players are still in the hand. You may want to save your 20 dollars and fold these cards.

But let's consider another scenario later in the evening. Again you have the last action, and again, you're staring at 7-8 with six other players still in for the pot. This time, though, the expert player and two of the guys at your level have folded; of the six contenders, only one of them is as strong as you. This is a time when you are likely to play this marginal hand, because all things being equal, you should be able to outplay the majority of your opponents.

Spotting the Novices

So how exactly can you spot the novices quickly? There are a few telltale clues that will send you a clear signal every time.

Dead Giveaways

Let's start with the simple stuff. That guy with the largest stack of chips who stole the blinds twice and won a decent-sized pot in the 10 minutes since you sat down? Odds are that he is probably not a novice. Same thing goes for the older woman who has folded every hand except an AK that gave her the two pair off the flop for a win.

If you play at the same casino or game room often and spot a couple of regulars sitting at your table, you obviously know that you can weed them out from the novice category as well. This is a good reason to play the same venues consistently if you are serious about your game, because it will help you not only identify the individual tells of opponents you see regularly, but also to select games with the highest percentage of new, and hopefully weak, blood.

> **Tilt**
>
> Although we focus specifically on novices in this chapter, we definitely don't mean to suggest that you shouldn't watch for tells of more experienced players. But right now you're focusing your efforts on identifying the weaker players at the table so that you can pick them apart first. We devote an entire chapter, Chapter 6, about spotting the subtler tells of poker pros.

Player Profiling

There's an old saying about never judging a book by its cover. However, that saying only partially applies to poker. Police and soldiers use "profiling" a great deal, and it's often a controversial subject because it uses specific markers for race, dress code, mannerisms, and so on, to "target" a specific group of people. Despite this, similar techniques are effective in certain situations when used correctly. You can use some similar techniques to separate the sharks from the suckers at the poker table.

We've already talked about certain people you can rule out right away. Let's say you've managed to categorize three people right away in the first few minutes of play—either you recognize them as regulars, or you know by them by the size of their stack and the effectiveness of their play.

This leaves you with six players whom you want to "profile" to gauge their skill. Here are some factors that might help:

- **Age.** Someone once said that old age and treachery will usually triumph over youth and strength. This is quite applicable to the game of poker. While we won't deny that there are plenty of good younger players in the game, if you see a guy sit down at the table in the Vegas and he looks about 21, wearing a college fraternity T-shirt, then it's quite reasonable to assume that he may well be an easier mark than the 40-something fellow on his right.

- **Gender.** Years ago, when poker was considered a "man's game," a female player would have been considered an easy mark. However—as co-author Bobbi wants to stress—that is no longer the case. Today, there are many very skilled female players, including poker champs like Annie Duke and Clonie Gowen. One thing to keep in mind: smart female players actually use the old-fashioned gender bias to their advantage. They're happy to let you underestimate their abilities—so they can outsmart you right out of that jackpot.

♦ **Sobriety.** At many casinos, players are treated to free drinks. Wow, these casino owners are pretty cool to be so generous, right? Not exactly. They have an ulterior motive. The reason behind the free drinks is to make you a looser player and a better mark for the slot machines and table games, where the house makes most of its money. That's good business for the casino, and bad business for the serious card player.

Now, in poker, you don't play against the house, and if you take advantage of those free drinks, chances are, you will help only your opponents. Don't drink heavily at the poker table, and regard anyone who does as a potentially weak player. Alcohol is a relaxant, and large quantities of it will dull perception and reaction speeds. In smaller quantities, an opponent may drink to calm his or her nerves and offset anxiety; in any event, be more concerned with a sober player than one who has put away several drinks.

The Importance of Associates

We've already framed poker as a war, and you don't usually go to war in a serious manner against your friends. Serious poker players are usually too focused on the goal at hand (winning) to risk being distracted by chatty pals. Plus, frankly, an intense poker player isn't likely to be great company. As a result, veterans tend to be like lone wolves. So if you see two or more friends or relatives, couples, or, especially, groups of three or more young men sit down at the table, then the odds are good that they are amateurs who are "playing for fun," which in our book translates to potentially easy marks.

One thing to remember is that—especially in a group of two people—there is the chance that they are playing together. This is definitely a sign of more experienced players, and also ones who are walking a fine line with regards to poker ethics. How can you tell the difference between a pair like this and the oblivious couple from Spokane who are just having fun in Vegas?

Look for the pair who are working in concert to sit across from each other, rather than side by side (assuming that there are open seats in both places.) Also, look for indications from their game play, such as one partner raising or re-raising off the other partner's bet to build the pot, and then folding or checking after other players have been forced out. And look for either partner checking around when it's just the two of them in the game. Are players like this cheating? No, but chances are, they are reading a set of tells off each other that no one else has spotted. They know when their partner is holding pocket Aces because of a certain look, or perhaps, because of an action with chips or the cards. The information is right there for anyone else at the table to see, but only if they know what to look for.

Tilt

If a pair of experienced players are working together, and both are in a hand, it's probably going to be dangerous and expensive to play—consider folding if you aren't holding the nuts. This is a topic we discuss more in Chapter 6 when we talk about expert players.

The Major Novice Tells

Profiling should give you a little head start, but you really want to try to spot an obvious tell to confirm that the player you are studying is new to the game.

There are four major signs to look for in a novice player. Typically, general anxiety or nervousness during the game is the biggest sign. The other three clues are repetitive betting patterns, quick reactions when betting, and indecisiveness prior to a fold.

Anxiety

Anxiety can manifest in many ways. Look for nervous behavior, such as tapping of fingers or feet, or any repetitive body-part movement. As we discussed previously, this indicates that the person is breathing faster than normal, and the body is trying to compensate and "burn off" some of the excess oxygen. Other signs of anxiety can include the following:

♦ Chain-smoking

♦ Chewing toothpicks or fingernails

♦ Rolling chips through the fingers, or repeatedly shuffling chips.

♦ Continually sipping a drink. If someone continually sips a drink, it can be an attempt to cure a dry throat.

Why do newer players get so wound up? A lot of it is because the game of poker forces them to go against some basic psychological programming not to lie that most people started learning from an early age. "Don't lie." You learned it as a child at home, at school, at church—you were taught that lying is wrong, and liars get punished. Even as adults it's programmed into you; lie to the boss? You get punished. Lie to your spouse? Again, you can expect an unpleasant reaction. Wondering if you'll be caught lying is often worse than the punishment you'll face.

Help Card _____

Most people dislike lying. That's why eye contact can be so revealing—people find it hard to look someone right in the eye while lying to him or her.

So now people try to play poker. This is a game where they feel *forced* to lie in order to win. They can't be honest about what cards they have, or they'll get eaten alive. So they usually try to employ a simple lie—"strong is weak, weak is strong"—but they're terrified that others will figure out their strategy. The worst is, of course, when they are trying to bluff "weak is strong."

Their conscious brain tells them to say and do the things that will make everyone else at the table believe the lie, but their bodies will subconsciously betray them because they're uncomfortable about deception.

Repetitive Betting Patterns

The second big clue to look for is repetitive betting behavior. We discuss this in Chapter 5, but for now, here's one familiar pattern that a novice bettor might display:

> *Raising Aces or Kings before the flop*—This is what the "book" tells you to do; it's like doubling down on 11 in blackjack. The idea behind this strategy is sound. You want to force weaker hands out early, hands that might connect for a straight, flush, or set. The problem with this is that if a player does it consistently, and every time he raises before the flop ends up showing AA or KK after the final bet, it's a dead giveaway to what he's holding.

Quick Reactions and Indecision

Finally, a novice's betting tends to have quick reactions and indecision on folds. The novice will probably try to act in the "strong is weak" strategy in a calling situation, and waver and pretend that she doesn't know if she should risk her chips. However, given an opportunity to bet or raise, the novice is often so eager to win that she will bet very quickly—possibly even holding the chips in her hand before her action.

Conversely, the new player may be truly reluctant to fold marginal hands. He generally knows that the hand is not strong, but he may find it difficult psychologically to throw away a small pair or straight draw, even if the board is showing dangerous cards, such as a potential flush or multiple face cards. So if you are faced with a player who plays "strong is weak" and acts indecisive just prior to throwing down pocket Aces, but this same player also wavers consistently before folding, it's probably a good indication that you are playing with a novice.

Put It All Together

Okay, let's put everything together and see if we can create a formula to identify inexperienced players.

First off, you want to identify weaker players to give yourself an edge when deciding whether to play a marginal hand, and also to know how to play a strong or weak hand.

Start by quickly "profiling" the other players at the table to try to narrow the field, ruling out the players who clearly have some experience. To do this, look for regular players in the game and evidence of strong play, such as large stacks of chips or multiple consecutive wins.

Now you can quickly judge the rest of the players for signs of inexperience, such as a lack of sobriety, playing with friends, or relative youth. If they meet any of these criteria, then focus on each one for 10 to 20 minutes to see if you can detect one of the novice tells to confirm that you are up against an inexperienced player; if you can't detect one, give your opponent the benefit of the doubt and class him or her as being on par with yourself.

Now, we just mentioned one of the keys to detecting any tell, and that is focus. Tells are all around you; but if that's where you're looking, you will never see them. Instead, you need to focus all your powers of observation on one individual for at least 10 to 20 minutes to detect an amateur, and possibly much longer if you're trying to detect the tells of a more experienced player. This is important, so much so that we continually reiterate it in this book, but for now, remember that you need to focus on each of the opponents whom you suspect of being novices for at least 10 minutes. If you detect a tell that confirms an amateur status, make a note of it; for example, if the player in seat two acts indecisive and calls anyway, and he's holding face cards, you then know he's a novice—then you can choose another suspected novice to watch.

Also categorize the player in seat two as an amateur when you decide when and how to play certain hands.

As you can see, this is a time-consuming process; if there are six possible novices at the table, it may take one to two hours just to observe them all and to decide if they are in fact new to the game, or if they simply have some eccentricities, such as heavy drinking, a youthful appearance, or a girlfriend playing with them.

However, you should be able to reap the benefits of your newfound knowledge much sooner than that, as you will have a good feeling within the first 10 minutes of who the dangerous players are at the table, and every 10 to 20 minutes you should learn at least one distinctive sign from a player which can cause you to call or fold.

And that's the whole purpose of learning tells. If you can make a few more good calls in a given game, thus winning a few more pots, and also fold a few more times than you otherwise might, saving you money on hands you would have otherwise lost, then you're going to find yourself making a lot more money at the game of poker in the long run.

The Least You Need to Know

- Learn to detect novice players quickly, and you can have a big advantage when you decide which games to join for the best odds of winning.

- There are several instant tip-offs—such as a large pile of chips—that a player isn't a novice.

- Novices fit certain profiling characteristics, such as being a much younger person or with a group of friends.

- Anxiety, nervousness, and repetitive betting are all among the most common—and most obvious—tells.

Chapter 4

The Most Basic Tells

In This Chapter

- Taking deception for granted
- Why the eyes are important
- Body-language basics

In this chapter, we cover the most basic and obvious poker tells. Most experienced players should be savvy enough not to show these dead giveaways, but you may spot these basic tells with newer players—or old pros who have simply let their guard down for a moment.

The Strong/Weak Deception

We will discuss three of the most basic tells: eyes, facial expression, and body language. But before we start with those, let's address a basic premise on which we are going to base a lot of our interpretations.

Because we know that we wouldn't tell someone the true value of our cards ("Wow, look at that … pocket Aces again!") unless we felt we had something to gain by such a declaration, then it's reasonable to assume that other players at the table won't either.

Instead, there's the "playing strong as weak, weak as strong" deception that players commonly practice. They attempt to disguise their strong hands as weak ones to lure unwary opponents into betting into them. Frequently they will hesitate before calling a bet, give pensive looks, and glance at their hole cards again. They try to draw out the bet to make it seem like they're making a tough and possibly bad decision to stay in the hand. In reality, they're hoping that someone with a decent hand will decide to raise again, giving them another opportunity for dramatics, or a chance to put the shoe on the other foot with a big re-raise, making their opponent suddenly doubt the strength of their hand.

The problem with this is twofold. First, if someone is playing "strong is weak, weak is strong" a lot, it's easy to gauge the strength of their hand just by applying inverse reasoning. Second, although a player may be deliberately acting strong or weak in a given situation, he or she will probably be giving off subtle tells that indicate the *true* strength of the hand. You want to learn how to detect these signals, because there are times when people will play strong because they *are* strong, and those are the hands you want to get out of early unless you're holding the strongest possible hand.

The big lesson to take away from this is to watch yourself to make sure you're not falling into the trap of playing "strong is weak, weak is strong" so often that other players at the table can read you.

So now let's talk about those tells that give us a better idea of the true strength of an opponent's hand.

It's All in the Eyes

It's been said that eyes are the windows to the soul, and, in fact, what people do with their eyes can give you a lot of information about the strength of their hand. Oftentimes opponents will disguise their eyes with sunglasses or a hat with a low visor, because they know that their eyes can be a powerful indicator for an observant student of the game.

HELP **Help Card**

Many top poker players frequently wear dark glasses while playing, to prevent their eyes from giving clues to their hand. For example, Greg "Fossilman" Raymer has become well-known for the cat-eye sunglasses he always wears during poker games.

Assuming that your opponents have not taken the drastic step of wearing glasses, what can we learn from watching their eyes?

Soldiers and cops often talk about the "thousand-yard stare." This is where a person is not really looking at you, but through you. They are in a world of their own, and may be unresponsive to conversations and other distractions. If they're in the hand, they've probably got good cards and are already raking in the pile in their mind.

Quite the opposite is the "target stare." You may get this at any time during the game, but it very often occurs when you are head to head. Your opponent's eyelids narrow, and he is looking directly at you. This is a hostile and aggressive move—not surprisingly, because you're the only thing standing between him and the pot. He may very well be a little insecure about his own hand and is now trying to intimidate you into folding.

Consider this; if your opponent were *holding the nuts*, would he bother staring you down? No, he'd just relax and get ready to collect the money. In fact, he'd be more likely to try to appear a little tentative in hopes of coaxing a raise or a re-raise out of you.

Another look that cops and soldiers are attuned to is the "target glance." This is a quick, furtive look directed toward an opponent's face. This indicates a player who is on the lookout for tells also, and it may cue you in to where the most experienced or dangerous players at the table are sitting.

Lucky Lingo

When a player has the best possible hand, he is said to be **holding the nuts.** The nuts is the best possible hand, and you can refer to it at any point in the hand. Preflop, it would be aces, although the term is more properly and commonly used by experienced players only after the flop, turn, or river. The term is said to come from the old west, when they used to take the nuts off of their wagon wheels to prevent theft. When a player bet the wagon's nuts he was betting the wagon, and would only do that with the strongest hands.

The Importance of Visual Clues

How important are visual cues? They're so important to interpersonal communication that we've developed a whole range of "smileys" or emoticons to complement our e-mails and text messages. Because, even between close friends, a simple sentence in black and white may sound sarcastic and hurtful unless it's accompanied by a little smiling face giving a conspiratorial wink. Suddenly, the sentence has been transformed into something funny, recalling a shared joke.

But when people are talking, we rely much less on these visual cues; instead, we look for changes in tone and inflection to tell us whether someone is angry, calm, joking, serious, and so on. Because we have a highly developed verbal language and rely on it so much as a species, we tend to be very "lazy" at using our eyes to read subtle nonverbal cues when people are talking.

Three Important Eye Movements

A trio of specific eye movements directed toward the player's hole cards can reveal the true strength or weakness of his or her hand. The most obvious is when the player seems focused on his or her hole cards. This strongly indicates a good hand. People often have a great desire to keep gazing at a big pair. It's akin to sifting through a big pile of chips or coins with your fingers; human nature is to want to reach out in touch, or in this case stare, at wealth, or potential wealth.

The second example of a significant eye movement is when a player checks her hole cards quickly after the flop. This usually means that the player is looking to see if she has made a straight. She saw the cards when they were first dealt, and knows that she has two unsuited cards, but can't remember both numbers. This is a sure sign of weakness; she is unlikely to forget that she just got dealt A-K (spades), but after getting 3(heart)-10(club) she might have to take a quick look after a 4-6-7 flop. Similarly, when the board shows a 3-card flush draw Q-2-9 (hearts), a player may look quickly to confirm which suits he's holding. In this situation, if the player bets as though he had the flush off the flop, it's almost certainly a bluff; he's most likely holding only one heart. Now, if another heart shows on the turn or river, and the player isn't holding a strong flush of his own (or something better), then he should fold and save his money.

Help Card

A doctor once told co-author Andy that he looks at the dilation of pupils to read his opponents. People's pupils dilate when they get excited, and it's a very difficult physiological reaction to control. This doctor's medical training and practice made him an expert at detecting this reaction. Similarly, Andy plays with a poker-playing movie actor/director who reads people by looking at their temples. He also gives false tells by controlling his own temples—a technique that he uses often in his work as an actor and director.

The third eye movement associated with the cards is to check the hole cards prior to calling a bet. This is an obvious "strong is weak" play. The key here is to look for other tells that indicate the player is feeling aggressive or dominant in spite of an attempt to mislead with an obvious clue. On the other hand, if body language is submissive or indicates that the player feels threatened, then the act of checking can be the clinching sign of a truly weak hand. Maybe the person is trying to decide whether to put up money to try to connect a straight or to look for a three-of-a-kind off a small pair.

Guarding Against Your Own Eye Tells

Now that you know some things to look for in others, don't forget that you want to ensure that you don't allow yourself to be easily read, either. Conceal your eyes behind a pair of comfortable glasses. This simple step will eliminate a lot of revealing cues. If playing a "strong is weak" position, ensure that your body language isn't dominant (we talk more about this in a little while.) Finally, use the "target stare" from time to time when you *do* have a strong hand. (Lower or remove your glasses for the maximum effect.) This may sometimes cost you 20 or 30 dollars in the pot, if your aggressive stance causes an opponent to fold earlier than he or she might have, but reveal your cards before you rake in the pot to make it clear that your stare is not a sign of weakness. This will throw a little confusion into your opponent's mind, and may enable you to bluff successfully using a similar stare later in the game.

HELP

Help Card _____

Don't look at your opponents in the eye unless you are trying to read them. To keep his eyes focused elsewhere, co-author Andy picks something on the ceiling or wall such as lights or ceiling tiles, and counts them to keep his eyes focused elsewhere.

Facial Expressions

Beyond just the eyes, the face itself can give the canny observer a wealth of information about his or her opponent's emotions. This is another reason to wear large glasses or a low-drawn cap, so that your face is covered as much as possible.

HELP

Help Card _____

If you're a man, and are truly serious about camouflaging your own facial tells, then consider growing a fairly full beard; this alone will conceal a multitude of subtle clues that your face could otherwise show.

Expressions Are Instinctual

Since the 1960s, the human face has been the study of numerous psychologists and anthropologists. Dr. Paul Ekman is a professor of psychology who is considered to be one of the top experts in the physiology of emotion and nonverbal communication. He conducted a famous study, published in *American Psychologist* magazine in 1993, to disprove the earlier beliefs that facial expressions were learned behaviors dependent on the culture in which a person was raised. By contrast, Dr. Ekman's study found that there were a host of emotions that could be universally inferred just by looking at a picture of someone's face.

From the rainforest of New Guinea to the concrete jungle of New York, primitive headhunters and professionals in three-piece suits could look at pictures and give the same answers. Smiling, with upturned corners of the mouth and eyebrows slightly raised, people universally interpreted as happiness; people interpreted frowns as sadness; clenched teeth, furrowed brows, narrow eyes meant that someone was angry. So in fact, these and many more expressions and their meanings are hardwired into us by evolution.

Bet You Didn't Know

Dr. Ekman's research described the importance of "micro-expressions." These are the instantaneous expressions that appear on a person's face—often only for a split-second—as soon as the person feels an emotion, often before the person is even consciously aware that he or she feels the emotion. Ekman believed that people are unable to mask or avoid giving off micro-expressions. But you have to be very observant in order to spot them!

For the poker player, the significance of this is threefold. First, these expressions, while they may be fleeting, are essentially an automatic reaction to emotion and will be visible unless someone is deliberately trying to control or disguise them. Second, because everyone is subject to these automatic reactions, we know that we need to do everything we can to disguise ourselves against those who may be watching us. Third, we know that we are genetically programmed not just to make these faces, but also to recognize them. Theoretically, then, there is nothing to keep us from reading our opponents like books, right? Unfortunately, it's not quite that simple.

Body Language

The person who is hemming and hawing over a seemingly weak hand might be betrayed by his or her body language. Certain body language is distinctive and recognizable in people who feel either dominant or aggressive in a situation. Other signs can indicate feelings of submission or fear, which the observant player can use to recognize when a strong play such as a check-raise or a re-raise may force an opponent to surrender a big pot.

Actions to Watch For

Telltale signs of a dominant, aggressive posture include leaning forward, or keeping hands raised at face level. Examples are people touching their temples with their fingers, stroking their chin, and so on.

A repetitive movement, such as drumming of the fingers, stroking the chin or beard, and shuffling or flipping chips, indicates the body's subconscious effort to burn off the excess oxygen being circulated through the bloodstream by the fight-or-flight response.

Folded arms are a classic sign of defensiveness, which translates into feeling threatened. This can be an indication of a weak hand or a reluctance to continue wagering on a particular pot. Arms that are folded or otherwise held close to the body can also indicate discomfort.

Help Card

Watch an opponent's head as other players are betting before your action. When chips are going into the pot, if the opponent gives a slight nod or shake of the head, often accompanied by a very faint smile, it's a good sign that the person has a strong hand. The side-to-side "No" motion is saying, "Nope, you didn't want to do that" as someone makes a bet. It's an unconscious I-told-you-so. Similarly, a nodding of "Yes" is a way of saying, "Yeah, come on, make my pot a little bigger."

Hunched shoulders create a submissive posture, indicating that an opponent is feeling generally beaten and "unlucky." When combined with a sad, drawn face over a period of time, and a small or shrinking chip stack, this body language can indicate that a player is *on the ropes* and will probably fold against strong play. On the other hand, if a player like this does stay in and bet strongly, then it's a good time to fold a marginal hand—the player has probably got a very strong hand.

Lucky Lingo

A player is said to be **on the ropes** if they are in a desperate position—in other words, backed into a corner.

Conversely, an erect posture, smiling face, and open arms can indicate a player who's "riding high" and may have a tendency to play a little fast and loose.

Body language is another evolutionary development that has given us a universal set of nonverbal cues to determine another person's intentions. This language predates the human race and can in fact be found in almost all species of animals. A dog shows submissiveness by the way he dips and turns his head, exposing his neck and then rolling over to offer his vulnerable belly in submission. On the other hand, we can all recognize an aggressive dog with teeth bared, a wide stance, head forward, and hackles raised. You don't need to hear this animal growl to know that she is challenging you. In fact, it's often easier to recognize the body language in the rest of the animal kingdom because we are not being distracted by verbal cues.

Body language in humans, like with other animals, developed as an evolutionary "safety valve" to reduce the amount of actual fighting for dominance over mates, food, and water. Fights like this did happen, but only as a last resort and usually by individuals or groups of equal strength. However, many fights—and much injury and death—are avoided by displays of aggression prior to any actual conflict, where individuals or groups attempt to scare their foe into flight or submission by trying to seem as large, aggressive, and threatening as possible. Bared teeth, wide stances, and large, violent movements are often used in these situations.

If one individual chooses to submit, rather than to fight or flee, then he uses another set of nonverbal signals to indicate that he is not a threat. Stillness, small, nonthreatening movements, hands out or palms up, are all very submissive signs. Touching the face or tugging at beard or hair are also signs that a person is willing to submit.

Putting It All Together

The basic premise behind why you study tells is to help you determine what your opponent is really holding. The key to successful poker play is not just knowing how to play your own hand, but also knowing how to play the opposition.

We know that most average players are going to employ a little acting and try to make you think that they're strong when they're really weak, and vice versa. However, we also know that this goes against some basic strategies of poker. One of the biggest of these is using the strength of good hole cards, like A-A, to force weaker hands out of the game before the flop, turn, or river in order to keep a weak hand from connecting late and ruining your play. Pocket Aces can be disappointing if players with a 2-3 off-suit hand aren't forced out and then pick up a 2 on the flop and another on the river. Suddenly you can find yourself check-raised and losing the pot to a hand that never should have played that far.

So how can you tell when your opponents really have strong hole cards, and are betting strong to force out weak hands, and when they actually *have* weak cards and are employing the basic misdirection strategy of "weak is strong?"

You look for tells that don't match the betting behavior. If a person is betting strong before the flop, and is telling everyone else to do themselves a favor and fold, but is sitting in a hunched position with crossed arms, and checks her cards right after the flop, then she's probably bluffing.

On the other hand, if a player is sitting in a relaxed and open position, smiling a little when players ante up, and bets strong before and after the flop without checking her cards, chances are good that she does in fact have a powerful hand.

Now, all you have to do is consider how your hand is going to play against whatevers she's holding. The player who is bluffing probably has, at best, a small pair, or, at worst, is working on connecting a straight or flush. Look and see if the board is showing either. Then, consider if your hand will beat whats she's holding.

In the case of the player who is honestly coming strong, you know that he's holding either a pair of Jacks or better. How do your cards stack up? This gives you the basis for deciding whether to bet or fold.

The Least You Need to Know

- In poker, always assume that everyone is lying or misleading you, and look for clues to help uncover the truth.

- The eyes are probably the single most important source of poker tells.

- Body language and expressions are instinctual, and can often be difficult—if not impossible—to control.

- You need to be observant and alert in order to spot split-second visual clues of your opponents.

Chapter 5

Subtle Versus Blatant Tells

In This Chapter

- Why subtle and blatant tells are important
- Common blatant tells
- Subtle tells to watch out for

Building the House of Cards

We've already discussed several different types of tells: physical tells, physiological tells, pattern tells, and speed tells. Some of these may be quite obvious, while others are considerably subtler.

In this chapter, we discuss several of the most blatant, as well as the subtlest, tells that are often encountered in the game of poker. Throughout this chapter, it's important to remember that in every situation, we start with the simplest observations, and build on that.

The House of Cards

Think of building a house; until you have laid a solid foundation and framed the walls, it's a bit early to worry about the color of the shingles. Consider identifying the novice and experienced players at the table as the foundation of your "house of cards."

Then add a basic frame and determine the playing styles of your opponents at the table. Who are the *fish*? Is there a *rock*? Which players are aggressive, and of these, who are the tight, dangerous players?

> **Lucky Lingo**
>
> In poker slang, a **fish** refers to a poor player or novice. Savvy poker veterans avoid upsetting the fish—or "tapping on the aquarium"—so that they won't leave the game, thus ending the opportunity to beat them. A **rock** is a player who is conservative and fairly predictable.

Finally, you are ready to put up the roof and walls, which is learning a simple set of blatant and subtle tells to determine what cards a certain player holds and how he or she is likely to play them.

Blatant Tells

Remember Teddy KGB eating his Oreos in the movie *Rounders*? He would separate and eat them in a certain way—until Matt Damon's character pointed out this obvious tell, prompting poor Teddy to fling his Oreos against the wall. Well, that was a pretty blatant tell. Unfortunately, it was a little too obvious; most of what we call blatant tells aren't going to be that obvious, and therefore, bad.

All types of players use blatant tells; some are specific in nature to a certain kind of person.

We discussed patterns of betting behavior, and if you can place an opponent in one of the five major categories, you should know what sort of cards the player holds by the way he or she has bet before and after the flop. You now need to watch for additional cues as to whether you should call, raise, or fold.

Why are you studying tells in the first place? The answer is simple: to become a better poker player and win more hands. The problem is, people equate winning with calling and raising. So inherently, you're going to look for tells that let you know when a player is weak, tells that give you an incentive to call or raise.

But perhaps even more important are the tells that show you when a player is really strong. It's important not to overlook or ignore these tells, because while it's nice to win a $200 pot, if you've lost three previous hands where you called for $60 before getting beat, you really haven't won much.

It's tempting to think that you can win every hand. And there's a little voice in the back of your head telling you that you can do it. But with nine other players at the table, statistics indicate that you're really only going to be able to win about 10 percent of the time.

The key is to lose less the other 90 percent of the time by knowing when to check or fold (or, if you have odds to call a bet, knowing when not to raise).

Signs That It's Time to Fold

With that said, let's talk about some blatant tells that send a clear signal that it's time for you to fold.

- **The Smiling Fish.** When a player you peg as a fish covers his mouth with his hand, he's probably trying to hide a smile. This is definitely a danger signal. It's unique to fish, because the other player types are generally too advanced to blatantly smile in the first place.

- **Sudden Alertness.** This is a blatant tell for all types of players, although it is likely to be most apparent in the rock. The rock will typically go the longest time between playing hands.

   If a rock raises preflop in no-limit and watches the flop closely, and then raises after the 9-J-A flop, you should think about folding an A-K and certainly fold anything worse. While you might not want to fold 9-9 or J-J, you should at least play cautiously. And if you have a flush draw or straight

draw, now would be the wrong time to try a
semi-bluff—just call if you have the right
odds, otherwise fold. For example, if you
had QcTc and there were two clubs on the
9-J-A flop, you have a better than 40 percent chance of beating a set of aces by the
river. Ordinarily, this would be a good spot
to try a semi-bluff, but if you read your
opponent for a strong hand that he won't
fold, you should just call instead.

Lucky Lingo

To **semi-bluff** is to bet or raise
before the river with a hand that is probably currently behind but has a good
chance at winning by the showdown.
Semi-bluffing is a powerful play, giving
you two ways to win. You can win when
your opponents fold, and you can win by
getting a little lucky if they happen to call.
When you don't pick up a tell, all your
big bluffs on the flop or turn should be
semi-bluffs.

Sudden alertness from a weak player seated
to your right in the same situation might clue
you in to a chance to bluff and possibly steal
the pot, or at the very least get a free draw.

On the other hand, if a weak player were to
re-raise against your re-raise, it would be
reasonable to fold the hand, because he

must have the Aces. You know this because if he's weak, he would only be confident enough to re-raise a hand with pocket Aces.

Bet You Didn't Know _____

Even a poker expert like co-author Andy sometimes needs to be careful to not exhibit tells. "After one event, I thought I might have been giving away tells, so I decided to try something different, and the next tournament I started to bend my head down and hide my face with my hands. If I had a really strong hand when there was betting after the flop (I never had top pair or better even once), I would have done the same thing. But after listening to comments from others and seeing myself on TV, I decided to change again. First, hiding my face like that made me look weak. Second, many people said that it didn't look good on TV. So lately I've been concentrating on my opponents and acting like they act. Sometimes I even mirror what they do, which I think helps me to read them by putting myself in their shoes (physically as well as mentally).

♦ **Abnormal Betting Behavior.** A blatant tell that should always get your attention is abnormal betting, especially by a rock, a tight aggressive, or a weak player.

If any of these players bets three or more consecutive hands, that's a good indication that something has changed. There are only two possibilities. The first, and least likely, is that he actually gets a run of premium cards. The odds are very much against that, which leads to the second, more likely possibility. The player is changing his style of play and you need to re-evaluate him when you decide what hands to play against him and how to play him.

Why Players Change Their Style

In the case of the tight aggressive player, she's probably playing looser for one of two reasons: The first is that the table may be tight, which will enable her to get away with looser play and make money doing so. This will probably happen at a table with a lot of tight aggressive players and rocks. It is unlikely to occur when there are several fish or loose aggressive players who keep the action going. Your response in this case would be to play a little looser yourself, taking a cue, as it were, from the tight aggressive player. In fact, if you've already "read" the table properly, you may already be playing a looser game than you normally would and be stealing a lot of small pots from the ultra-conservative players.

Bet You Didn't Know

In tournaments, you'll see players change their styles frequently as their stacks fluctuate and the tournament gets closer to jumps in the prize money. A player who was playing loose and aggressive with a big stack may tighten up after losing a few pots, and a tight player may try to steal more pots after going on a rush and becoming the chip leader at the table. Most players will tighten up when they are close to the prize money (no one wants to go out on the "bubble", one spot from the money). Some players will use that as a signal to start stealing as many pots as possible. After the money is reached, most players will loosen back up.

In long, multi-day tournaments, players will tighten up just before the dinner break and the end of play for the day (unless they are low on chips and want to gamble to avoid having to come back the next day). And you'll often see players just back from a dinner break get overaggressive and bluff off all their chips.

The second reason why a tight aggressive might loosen up is simply to throw his opponents for a loop. Remember, the way that you're trying to play should get you categorized as a tight aggressive player yourself, especially if you're too consistent. That's why you want to try to switch up your game a little every now and then to keep everyone at the table guessing. If they don't have a good feel for what cards you are likely to play, then they won't be sure how to play you. So at a table that contains all types of players, a tight aggressive going on a short run of raising and calling can indicate that he is trying to fool the rest of the players into thinking he's a loose aggressive player. Then, when he goes back to playing only premium hands, people aren't going to be as threatened by his action and will tend to bet into him more readily. At this sort of balanced table, you're not going to bite. You'll keep playing only the best cards against those players who you've typecast as tight aggressives, and fold any time you think they have you beat.

Help Card

A reminder: a tight aggressive is a player who is selective about the hands he plays— but then plays very aggressively. A loose aggressive is similar, but they play too many hands—making it likely they'll be a losing player.

When a weak player starts playing a lot of hands, it means just one thing: He's beginning to act like a fish, a weak fish. People who have a habit of folding against pressure will continue that habit whether they're playing one good hand every 20 minutes or 5 marginal ones in the same timeframe. You can play this like it is: an opportunity to make even more money off this person. You can play marginal hands against them if there aren't other, more dangerous players in the pot, and rely on bluffing to force them out of the money. You still want to look for hands strong enough to beat them if they try to go to the river with a small pair or similarly weak cards.

A rock who begins to play a looser game is probably on tilt. This rarely happens with the tight aggressive opponent. It's more likely to happen with the weak player, or the rock. In this case, you can open up and play a little looser against this opponent, and know that her angry and unfocused behavior means that she's no longer playing the premium cards that you would normally associate with calls and raises.

The other two types, loose aggressive and the fish, play so many hands that it's harder to tell what is "abnormal" for them, but there is one sure sign to look for: If either of these players stops playing almost every hand, then it is a sign that he may be tightening up his game. If this happens when his bankroll appears low, for instance, few chips in front of him, then it may simply be a response to the dwindling stack of chips. Consider treating his next few hands with respect, as he is probably going to try to play only premium cards. If he hits a couple of pots and goes back to betting every hand, then return to the strategies that we previously outlined.

Subtle Tells

Let's return again to the movie *Rounders*. In one scene, Matt Damon's character walks into a judges' weekly poker game and tells each player what he's holding after watching the game for a few minutes. Well, that's the movies. In real life, you shouldn't be that concerned with *what* any particular player is holding—you just want to be able to tell whether your hole cards will beat theirs. You need to watch for the more subtle tells—as this is the key to successful poker. We will go into more detail about various subtle tells in Chapters 6, 7, and 8.

Help Card

Could you expect a call to be very easy most of the time? No, probably not. If you use our system of tells to help you decide with conviction whether to bet or fold between 60 percent and 80 percent of the time, you'll be doing well. The rest of the time you're going to have to trust your gut and instinct, or pick up on the subtler tells of your opponents. Subtle tells are usually variations on some of the basic ones we discuss earlier in this book.

The Quick Peek

Quickly peeking at hole cards after a flop generally indicates a player checking for a straight or a flush.

Strong betting after a straight flop indicates a made hand. If it's a flush flop, she is probably still looking for another suited card on the turn or river, because if she had a flush draw, she wouldn't have to peek.

Smiling

Smiling while checking or calling is a common tell. Remember, we said that a lot of facial expressions are subconscious; people often don't even know that they are making them. The facial expressions are just an instinctive reaction to a good or bad stimulus. In poker, the only *real* reason to check or call is if you are holding a draw hand; if your hand is made, the *real* action should be to raise. But, of course, if you are slow-playing a made hand and are trying to build the pot, then you're going to *act* like you are playing a draw—hence, the check or call. But a draw hand is not a positive stimulus; it's an unknown, and if anything, should create anxiety. Will you get the cards you need? Expect an inquisitive or anxious expression. Instead, your opponent is showing a slight smile, leading you to believe that his hand is not a draw, as his action suggests, but is in fact a made hand. Now take that into account when deciding how to play your hand.

Head Movements

Shaking or nodding of the head are good indicators to fold a marginal hand. These are both unconscious signs that an opponent is holding good cards.

We discuss more tells involving body language, food, drink, chips, and even conversation in Chapters 6, 7, and 8. For now, it's enough to say that you should strive to use the biggest tells most often, which are player skill levels and style of play. If you're still not sure, then look for a blatant tell, such as abnormal betting behavior. And finally, if all else fails, focus on a particular opponent and see if you can detect a subtle tell, such as a slight smile or a peek at his hole cards, to let you know how to play against him.

The Least You Need to Know

+ A successful player needs to recognize both subtle and blatant tells.

+ Many tells signal that a player's hand is weak, but you also need to watch for tells of a strong hand.

+ Common blatant tells include smiling, sudden alertness, and abnormal betting behavior.

+ Subconsciously smiling and slight head-shaking at certain points in the game are examples of subtle tells.

Chapter 6

Tells of the Pros

In This Chapter

- Why the flop is a critical time
- Telltale signs of a fake-out
- Figuring out when to fold

Okay, so we've shown you how to classify players according to their poker personality, and you know how to identify the novices and spot their tells. Now it gets a bit tougher. At this point, you need to know how to spot tells of players who aren't new to the game. This chapter shows you how to identify clues from the more savvy breed: people who are sophisticated enough not to broadcast dead giveaways about their hand.

Who Is a Pro?

Before we look at how to spot the tells of professional players, we need to define what we mean by "professional."

The traditional definition of a professional poker player is someone who makes all or part of his or her living off winnings at the poker table. For our purposes, this definition may not be sufficient; let's also include all players who play at a level comparable to, or above, your own.

> **Bet You Didn't Know**
>
> One of the biggest—and most talked about—jackpot in recent history was won by Chris Moneymaker. He was an unknown accountant who won entry into the 2003 World Series tournament by way of a $40 satellite win. He ended up winning the big jackpot—$2.5 million.

Observation Is Critical

The key to picking apart a professional player's game is observation. Now, oftentimes if there is a single strong player at your table, and several weak, loose, or novice players, you can save a lot of trouble—not to mention money—simply by not playing against the heavy hitter.

And in poker, a dollar saved is a dollar earned. However, you do not always have this luxury; your position relative to the button may require you to bet before you see the professional's first action, or you may be at a table with several high-caliber players.

Finally, you do not want to give up some good pots; whatever the case for playing against this opponent, you need to respect his skill level while searching for chinks in his armor and exploiting any weakness you find.

Bet You Didn't Know

Some people are surprised by the sudden popularity of TV poker shows. Co-author Andy thinks it's a trend long over-due. "I always thought that if golf and bowling were watchable on TV, poker was a no-brainer if handled the right way. It's continuing to grow, and may eventually become more popular on TV than some major sports like football or basketball."

Watching the Flop

The most important time to watch your opponents is as the flop appears. Stand back and watch a game in progress sometime; notice where everyone is looking when the cards are laid out. More than 90 percent of the players are watching the flop—few people look at their opponents' faces.

Those cards will be there in 30 seconds, one minute, two minutes. That's plenty of time for you to look at them and decide what you're going to do, even if you have the first action. On the other hand, you'll never get truer information from players' facial expressions and body language than when they see the flop for the first time. It's like that old expression. You never get another chance to make a first impression. Only in this case, you're not worried about making a first impression, but rather, about *seeing* a first impression. Remember, we told you earlier in this book that there are automatic split-second facial reactions that most people can't control. That's what you need to look for, so training yourself to quickly watch opponents' faces—rather than watching the flop—can give you a valuable advantage.

> **Help Card** _____
>
> Given the choice, you want to focus on the strongest player at the table; if he's already folded, then concentrate on the next most dangerous individual. As you get better at scanning the players, you'll start to pick up on other people's actions from your peripheral vision. But pay the most attention to the greatest threat.

Here are three key indicators to look for as the flop is laid out.

The Player Perking Up

If a player suddenly shows interest in the game, take note.

A professional player may be relaxed and willing to wait for a good set of hole cards to come along. But it's only natural to betray your interest when you see your strong hole cards connect on the flop. Straightening up her posture, glancing at her opponents, touching her chips, are all indicators that a player may have just received a good hand.

A Quick Glance at Chips

If a player shoots a quick glance at his chips, this is another sure-fire indication that a strong opponent has picked up a powerful hand off the flop. You already know that most players will look at the flop; if a player glances quickly at his chips before he looks back at the board, or looks away, then you can be certain that you need a good hand to compete with him.

Double-Checking Hole Cards

The last thing you look for is a sign of weakness. Suppose you notice a player watching the flop, and then quickly peeks at her hole cards before she looks back at the board. If this happens, take a look at the board for a flush or straight draw. If it's showing, then you can safely figure this player for having four cards, but not the whole enchilada. Bet accordingly.

Spotting the Fake

The big difference between a professional player's bluff and the common bluff of the loose aggressive is that you respect the pro's play more.

If you've identified another player as a loose aggressive, you know that he will commonly raise with small or nonexistent hands and scare other players out of the pot. Thus, with a marginally strong made hand or a decent draw hand, you should tend to call the loose aggressive players a lot. On the other hand, the professional player uses the bluff for two reasons. The first is to keep his opponents off-balance; if he bluffs, is called, and loses in a showdown, gullible players may be inclined to think he's playing a looser game, and won't be as scared of him when he is actually playing a strong made hand.

The second reason is to capitalize on any fear that his tight playing style has instilled in wiser players. Anyone who has been paying attention to the tight aggressive professional has probably noticed that he hasn't played many hands, but almost every time he did, he won the showdown with powerful cards. Observant players like this tend to respect this player if he's in a hand, and this gives him the opportunity to steal a few pots. So, how do we tell when this cool cucumber is bluffing? This is critical, because if you can't get a good read on his bluff, then you have to play selectively and save your money if you don't have a very strong hand.

The following sections discuss five major indicators that a professional is trying to bluff you, listed in order from the most easily observed to the subtlest.

Betting Out of Turn

This is a blatant move intended to intimidate the person who's got the action *ahead* of the bluffer. The fact that she's moving a couple of stacks of chips forward, and looking like she's not only about to call, but in fact raise, will probably discourage a lot of players from making or calling a bet. And that's exactly what the pro wants to do, because she actually holds weak cards and is just trying to scare opponents out of the pot.

Exaggerated Movements While Betting

This is another fairly blatant attempt to discourage other players from calling; this time, it's aimed at anyone acting *after* the bluffer. By tossing chips with authority, or even flicking them into the pot, the pro is trying to send a strong message: "I've got this hand made." He doesn't. Call or raise.

The Stare-Down

If the player begins to stare at the bettor, take note. This is another obvious intimidation ploy, often seen when players are heads up. The pro is trying to make the bettor nervous, which is a sure sign that he doesn't have good cards; otherwise he'd want you nice and relaxed and betting into him.

Staring at the Board

This is a subtler attempt to make you think that he has such good cards that he just can't stop staring at them.

Covering Mouth with Hand

You may notice that the veteran will put her hand over her mouth. The professional has played enough poker to know that this is an amateur move that subconsciously indicates a good hand. She's using it to make you *think* her hand is stronger than it is. Don't be fooled.

Bet You Didn't Know

Even a poker expert like co-author Andy sometimes needs to be careful about not exhibiting tells. "After one event, I thought I might have been giving away tells, so I decided to try something different, and the next tournament I started to bend my head down and hide my face with my hands. Had I ever had a really strong hand when there was betting after the flop (I never had top pair or better even once), I would have done the same thing. But after listening to comments from others and seeing myself on TV, I decided to change again. First, hiding my face like that made me look weak. Second, many people said that it didn't look good on TV. So lately I've been concentrating on my opponents and acting like they act. Sometimes I even mirror what they do, which I think helps me to read them by putting myself in their shoes (physically as well as mentally).

Knowing When to Fold

You now know when to call a bluff, which is great. But even more important than that is to know when to fold a fairly strong hand, because a professional is trying to coax you into calling or raising.

Consider this situation. You hold A-K and the flop comes down A-5-K. After the first round of bets there are four players left in the hand: you, a loose aggressive player, a fish, and the only other strong player at the table. The weaker players at the table shouldn't be your prime concern. Consider what cards the strong player holds. You can safely assume that he would open with hole cards of Jacks or better, but if he's in the hand after the flop, you have to revise your assumptions. Would you try to bluff against a strong player with the board showing Aces and Kings? Okay, he probably won't either. That means he has one of the following three hands: A-K, K-K, or A-A. Notice that two of his possible hands will beat you, and one of them will end with you splitting the pot. This is already a dangerous hand in which to play, because you're looking at a slim chance of winning. But many people are going to fixate on their strong 2 pair, start thinking about the chance of making a full house, and will tend to call without considering the possible consequences.

Instead, you should concentrate less on your hand and try to figure out what your opponent's hand is. If he has the A-K, you should realize that he's in the same position as you are. If he has the first action, he's got to bet; if he checks, then assume his cards are strong and fold early, therefore costing him money. What you are looking for when he bets is any sign of weakness, a sign that you can be almost certain will be false, and meant to reassure you that it's okay to cover his bet, maybe even raise. If you see one of these faked signs of weakness, definitely peg him for having K-K or A-A.

Now, let's say he bets without making any obvious tells.

The turn card is a King. Now this player checks. Before your action, consider what cards he can possibly play. You should deduce now that he's either got the A-K or A-A; pocket Kings are out because you can account for three of them now.

A check is a definite indication of weakness, and is an invitation to raise and force your opponent out of the pot. But in this case, any bet on your part only sets you up for a check-raise and a costly loss if he is holding Aces, or has your money returned to you if you split the pot on A-Ks. Checking around is definitely the right thing to do.

Had your opponent raised, you'd again look for an indication of weakness as she raised—a slight shrug of the shoulders, hesitation in making the bet, and so on. If you saw anything like this, fold. Why? Because your opponent is trying to encourage your call. The only reason you'd have stayed in the hand if she had checked would be because it didn't cost you anything.

There's no sense calling two raises just to get to the showdown, even if you are holding Kings full of Aces. Not if your opponent is holding Aces full of Kings, which is what a hesitant bet like that should lead you to believe.

You can see that in this situation, it's hard for anyone to make money off these good cards. You figure out with a good degree of accuracy what cards she probably has in her hand, and do so quickly. Refine your selection down to just two hands, but notice that at no time after the flop did you have more than a 25 percent chance of winning.

The problem is that it's extremely difficult for even good, disciplined players to throw away a full house. In such a scenario, you should carefully watch your opponent for the slightest sign that you should fold, and that's where your knowledge of tells comes in.

Following are three solid indications that you are slowly drawn into betting a losing hand, and that it's time to fold.

Shrugging

A pro might pretend to indicate weakness with a slight shrug while making a bet. Have you ever done something that wasn't really smart, and when someone asked you why, all you could do was shrug? That's what this tell is trying to convey; the pro is trying to say, "Hey, I know this isn't a good call, but I'm going for it anyway." He wants you to read him as weak and foolish, and feel comfortable calling or raising. Don't. Unless you have the nuts, this would be a great time to fold.

Hesitating

This is another classic sign of weakness, and if you saw it in a novice player, you might rightfully assume that he really *didn't* know whether he should call, raise, or fold. With the pro, it's just too obvious that he's only trying to make you *think* he's weak. Don't buy it.

Folding out of Turn

If the pro starts to fold out of turn, it's possibly the most blatant attempt to lure the player acting ahead of the pro to call or raise. The pro picks up her hole cards, maybe with a regretful glance, and is holding them as if she's about to muck her hand. You are expected to feel relief that your best competition is throwing in the towel. She isn't, but unless you have the nuts, you probably should.

Now we've shown you how to get a good read on professional poker players, those who play at or above your own level. To re-cap, when possible, avoid playing against these individuals, but if forced to, then follow these guidelines:

- ◆ Watch them as the flop is dealt to pick up on their subconscious signals.
- ◆ Beat their bluffs by reading their fake "strong" tells.

   ◆ Be willing to fold even strong cards if their
     "weak" tells indicate that they have the nuts.

In upcoming chapters, we tell you about secrets of
body language, and how to capitalize on the power
of the spoken word.

The Least You Need to Know

   ◆ If at all possible, the smartest thing to do is
     simply avoid playing against opponents who
     skills are better than or equal to yours.

   ◆ Get in the habit of watching opponents'
     faces immediately after the flop appears.

   ◆ Clues that a pro is trying to bluff you
     include suddenly betting out of turn, staring
     at the bettor or board, and covering his
     mouth with his hand.

   ◆ Make sure you know when to fold if you
     suspect that you're drawn into betting a los-
     ing hand.

7

Body Language

In This Chapter

- Signals of smart players
- The vital skill of listening
- Important verbal clues

When you're sitting at the poker table, you can tell your opponents a lot about your hand without ever saying a word. In this chapter, we delve into more detail about how to read tells related to body language.

The Importance of Body Language

We already talked a little about the importance of body language, but this is such an important area of nonverbal communication that we take a closer look at it now. Much of what we discussed earlier were subconscious tells—the body language that most people don't even realize they are sending out. Now, we're going to study the "acted" tells, body language that smart players use to try and fake you into making a bad call or folding against a bluff.

We also talk about, well, talking. What to say, and what not to say at the poker table, and how to pick up on the conversational clues that other people may be giving away to anyone who knows what to listen for.

A Quick Review

It's been a while since we discussed these important types of tells, and our previous mention of this subject focused mainly on the scientific background of why people give off such a wealth of nonverbal information with their bodies. This chapter focuses on the specific tells you can read from body language, what they mean, and how they should affect your card play.

Let's quickly review what you already know. Body language tells are generally subconscious in nature, which means that they paint a very good picture of a player's true mental state.

A dominant, aggressive posture—shown by leaning forward, touching the temples with the fingers—when coupled with a "weak" tell, like looking unconcernedly away from the action and the board, is a sure sign that the player has strong cards.

His conscious mind is telling him to try to deceive his opponents by appearing uninterested, but subconsciously his body is preparing for combat.

HELP   **Help Card** _____

Any time you see a subconscious tell that conflicts with an acted tell, choose your play based on the subconscious action. In this case, it's an easy call to fold unless you have a strong hand.

You might have been worried by the apparent non-chalance of this player, but that coupled with his dominant body posture tells you that he really *is* a serious threat.

Body Language Tells of Smart Players

Now that we've reviewed the basics of subconscious body language, let's get to the real meat of this chapter: learning how to read the tells that your smarter opponents will "act out" to try to convince you to call when you should fold, and vice versa.

Shrugging

Coming from any player, you should consider a shrugging motion of the shoulders as a cue to fold. This may appear as an obvious shrug from a novice player or the slightest upward movement of the shoulders in a more experienced player. Shrugging is a sign of indecisiveness, and the "actor" is trying to convince you that she's betting against her better judgment, and that it's safe for you to call. She isn't and it isn't. Fold unless you're holding a very good hand.

Hand Near Mouth

Remember the Smiling Fish from Chapter 5? When he put his hand over his mouth, it meant that he was trying to conceal a smile indicating good cards. You believed this, because the Fish is such a poor player. On the other hand, if you saw a tight aggressive player perform the same action, you can be pretty sure she is bluffing. She wants you to think she has strong cards, but she doesn't. Call this tell.

Feigned Boredom

If a pro player is out of a hand and appears bored, staring off into space, you wouldn't pay much attention. For one thing, he isn't in the hand, so you need to focus on watching other opponents instead. And besides, you know how boring it used to be when you got a run of bad hole cards and didn't play for a dozen hands in a row. Notice we say how boring it *used* to be, because now you're using all that time when you aren't in a hand to study the other players at the table, right? Right. Now, if this player is *in* the hand and still appears bored and distracted, don't be fooled. He's got good cards and doesn't want to scare off the competition by appearing focused on the game. Play your hand accordingly.

Looking Away After Flop

A very similar tell is the player who watches the flop, and then quickly glances away and avoids eye contact with the other players at the table. Chances are good that he has connected on a strong draw hand or improved his made hand. Fold if you don't have a good hand of your own.

Boisterous Betting

Any time you see a player using exaggerated motions while she bets—like sweeping her arm in a wide arc, or flipping her chips into the pot—you should assume that she is bluffing. She's hoping that these aggressive motions spook players who may be undecided about betting or folding. If the actor really had good cards, she'd want as many players to stay in the hand as possible, and would be betting with more subtlety, or even faking hesitation. So unless you've got a strong hand, now would be a great time to fold and save some money.

The Sounds of Poker

It's amazing how much you can learn just by listening to what's going on around you at the poker table. Even more amazing is how much you can influence other players using the most innocent of questions and phrases.

Here's something that probably won't shock you: People love to hear themselves talk. And they love to talk about themselves! You are no exceptions to that rule, so the first thing you need to remember about verbal exchanges at the poker table is that you always want to be in charge and on your toes. If another player gets you talking about what you do for a living, your family, your worst bad beat, then two things are going to happen.

The first is that you're going to lose your focus on the game. You're going to turn inward, gathering up fresh material to wow your audience with. Unfortunately, your audience is just trying to distract you from what's going on at the table! The second thing that will happen is you'll start tuning in more to your conversation, and losing your focus on the nonverbal cues from players around you. Remember how we previously discussed the importance of nonverbal aspects of communication, and observed that once people start talking, their natural "laziness" comes into play and they listen only to the words?

Now, this doesn't mean you're going to play silently. On the contrary, you're probably going to talk a good bit, but you want to control the conversation, and you want to use your words to make your opponents feel more comfortable playing against you, or maybe to encourage a bad call.

Two Types of Talking Personalities

You want to make sure that you aren't falling into one of the two basic types of players who really stand out conversationally at the poker table: the strong, silent type and the chatterbox.

The Strong, Silent Type

This is the guy who sits there for an hour and says nothing. Asks for a drink, grunts when he loses a hand, maybe chuckles when he wins one. Other than that, nothing. You'll probably find that this person is also a conservative bettor, either a rock or possibly a tight aggressive.

> **Tilt**
>
> Don't expect to learn much from the few verbal clues of the strong, silent type. But remember, just because she's not talking doesn't mean she's not listening. So watch your own verbal clues.

You can still influence his betting decisions with your own words, but you don't want to direct any small talk his way, because it will just make you appear annoying. Sort of like this next character.

The Babbling Chatterbox

This is the person at the table who will not shut up. No matter what someone says, this player has an opinion. He'll talk to or at anyone, whether he or she is interested or not. When he leaves or takes a break, the other players may let out audible sighs of relief—and a silent prayer that he doesn't come back. Now you can play a little poker in peace! Needless to say, this is not the person you want to be.

Instead, you want to apply a soft touch. You want to talk only when you have something to gain. If some guy comes to the table where you're playing and behaves like a jerk, then you're going to resent losing money to him. And you won't be alone. Everyone else at that table will feel the same way. Because he's not likable. He doesn't tip the dealer, he laughs at opponents when he's taking their money, he hollers at the waitress, he makes fun of the new guy's bad call. What's going to happen? He's going to become the focus of every player at that table. If they go in on a hand, they're not playing against each other, they're playing against him. Everyone wants to see him lose, and it doesn't matter who beats him.

Why did this happen? Because, by his actions, words, and body language, he made himself a target. People began to feel bad about losing money to him, and decided to do something about it.

In contrast, consider how the soft touch would work. He's playing at your table again. He's polite to the waitresses and dealers, he tips when he wins. When he beats someone in a showdown, he offers a little consolation on his or her bad beat, or tells the person he just got lucky, and that if he'd been smart, he would have folded on the turn. When he loses a hand, he congratulates his opponent, shaking his head like he can't believe how dumb he is.

Bet You Didn't Know

Hardly anyone talks at a poker table more than Mike "The Mouth" Matusow. Co-author Andy used to hate playing with him so much that he'd ratchet up his play if Matusow sat down and leave if he was the slightest bit tired or for any other excuse. But Matusow learned that being so talkative—to the point that you motivate your opponents to play better—is counterproductive. There's a fine line, and if you don't know where it is, you're better off keeping relatively quiet. Andy doesn't have the same verbal skills as Matusow so he'll usually err in the other direction and keep mostly quiet, (but he's a Mike Matusow compared to a Howard Lederer or Chris Ferguson).

You're much more likely to see him as a "nice guy"—not a threat—maybe even someone to be pitied. People don't feel so bad when they lose to him, and as a result, they will lose more. Their level of play isn't as focused in his direction; if it's just him against another player in a pot, the other person may feel comfortable playing weaker cards.

Bet You Didn't Know

You also don't want to talk so much that you give away your hand. Andy was at a table with Matusow during a preliminary World Series of Poker tournament in 2005, and watched Matusow make a big bet and induce a call from his opponent on the river. Matusow rattled off a list of all the strong hands he didn't have. The board was something like A-T-7-6-2 and Matusow said, "I don't have the straight, I don't have 2-pair, I don't have a set of 2s, a set of 6s, a set of 7s ..." skipping the set of tens but covering all the other strong hands. If you were at the table and concentrating, you knew that Mike had trip 10s. His opponent didn't catch it and called with one pair. Maybe Matusow had said too much if he was against Andy, but when Matusow is playing well, his brain moves quick enough that he probably knew just enough to say to that particular opponent. Talking your opponent into making a mistake without giving away your hand is skill that's hard to learn, and best left to the Mike Matusows of the poker world.

The Middle Ground

We've discussed the two extreme types of talkers, but most players will fall somewhere in between these two ends of the spectrum. In that case, you'll need to work a little harder and be very observant. Now you're looking for not so much a specific action, but rather a change in behavior. If a person who had been fairy chatty suddenly clams up, for example, it may be a signal that you need to pay attention to this player.

Important Verbal Clues

Now that you know what you should be saying at the table, let's talk about what to listen for. There are three major verbal clues to look for.

Sighing

Whenever you hear a sigh after the flop, or before a call, you can be sure that the person making the noise is trying to mislead you into thinking that her cards are weak. Fold unless you have a powerful hand. The same thing goes for this next clue.

Sudden Silence

This will be noticeable in two cases: the babbler who suddenly shuts up, or the person who has been humming or whistling softly to herself for the last 20 minutes who just went mute. The reason behind both of these sudden silences is simple: The player is now concentrating on her cards and has unconsciously shut down her soundtrack. This is a powerful verbal tell, alerting you that something important has happened—the player's luck has taken a major turn, either for the better or worse.

> **Bet You Didn't Know**
>
> Showing your opponent your hand to gauge their reaction can be so powerful that most major tournaments have a rule that prohibits even telling your opponent what your have. The rule and its enforcement are often controversial. In some tournaments you can't tell the truth about your hand, but you can lie about it, and you can usually get away with saying something about your hand as long as you don't reveal its exact strength.

Asking a Dumb Question

Suppose you hear someone ask, "How much can I raise?" This is a common verbal tell. In fact, it's so common that you've probably done it yourself at some point. The player asking the dealer this question usually does so with a quizzical look on his face. They also usually do it while holding the nuts. This is just an attempt to look weak and "dumb" and to encourage other players to call the bet or the raise. Don't do it!

Here are some other common examples that fall under the same umbrella of dumb questions/statements:

- "Hey, you got a pair?"
- "C'mon, just give me the card."
- "You got the straight?"

I can think of many situations in which people use verbal cues, some of which may be bluffs, but all of which we should bring up. For example:

- C'mon, give me the card.

- So, you holding a pair?

- Is your pair bigger than mine?

- You got the straight?

- People also comment on others' people play.

- Gonna show us your hand if I fold?
  Whatcha got?

The Least You Need to Know

- You can learn a lot about an opponent's hand by reading his or her body language.

- Dominant posture coupled with a weak tell is often a sign of a strong hand.

- Sudden silence is an important clue about your opponent's hand.

- If your opponent is one of the two extreme types of talkers, you can have an advantage in reading their tells.

Chapter 8

Tells Involving Props

In This Chapter

- Why smokers give off more tells
- How food and beer can help you
- Several tells that involve handling chips and cards

Facial expressions, body posture, hand movements, and betting patterns are just a few of the many tells that the discerning poker player can pick up and use to his advantage.

Many more tells can be seen by watching the way a player handles her food, drink, chips, and cards. If and how a player utilizes a comfort item, such as a lucky coin or a teddy bear, can be yet another clue.

In this chapter, we discuss the major tells that utilize these types of props, how to pick up on them, and of course, how to guard against them.

Cigars, Cigarettes, and Toothpicks

If you're ever playing poker with smokers, you may be able to pick up on some telling behavior. A player makes a bet or calls a raise, takes a deep drag on his cigar, and lets out a big puff of smoke. Is this player bluffing? Probably not. This action is an indication that a player is very comfortable with the wager he just made.

Chain-smoking is cigarette-specific behavior that will indicate general nervousness in a player. Like excessive drinking, any over-the-top use of substances, including nicotine, is a sign of a tendency toward loose play.

There are other cigarette-related tells that can signify nervousness—creating smoke signals, for example, or doing other fancy tricks with cigarette smoke.

Another nervous behavior is playing with a toothpick. Like many other nervous behaviors, it can be the result of boredom. If the toothpick stops moving suddenly, watch out. This is a sign that the player is suddenly paying more attention to his cards and less attention to his nervous habit.

Food and Beer

We've already discussed the phenomenon of heavy drinking at the poker table, and what it means to you—a weak player who's ready to lose his bankroll. Let's talk about a couple of other food- and drink-related tells and what they mean.

Most casinos and card rooms will serve food at the tables. If a player is out of the hand and is working away at her steak and potatoes, it won't raise your eyebrows. On the other hand, if the same player is *in* the hand and still enjoying her meal, calling bets or raising, you can be very certain that she has a very good hand, and hence is comfortable eating because she doesn't feel obliged to pay attention to the board or her opponents.

Remember the cigar smoker who took a big drag and let it out? A similar tell would be a player who took a particularly long draught of beer and let out a satisfied "Aaahhh …" afterward. Such a player probably has strong cards and is unlikely to be bluffing, so play your hand accordingly.

These are some examples of confidence tells, but there are also some food-related tells that can be signs of nervousness or anxiety. If a player begins nervously chewing on ice or frantically stirring their drink with a straw, this can be a telltale signal that they're worried about their hand.

Comfort Items

Remember the old Peanuts cartoon, where Linus insisted on carrying his "security blanket" around everywhere?

Many card players also have a "lucky item" and you can use this to your advantage. First off, displaying of a good luck charm is a good sign that a player is weaker, and believes that poker is a game of luck, as opposed to skill. This is good, as it means that the player is less likely to know things like comparative hand strength, calculating pot odds, etc.

A common example of a lucky item would be a coin, like a silver dollar. Watch and see if the player uses this to protect his hand from time to time. (As we explained in a previous chapter, players frequently use chips or other items to protect their cards from being fouled or mucked.) If the player only protects *some* hands in this fashion, it almost always means that those are strong cards.

Chips

Players can give away a lot of information by the way they handle their chips. Everything from the way they stack their chips to when and how they play with them.

Generally, the loose aggressive players display an unorganized mass of chips, while the tight players and the rocks keep their chips stacked in neat, tidy columns. If you've ever seen a player who has not only stacked her chips, but lined up all the stripes, you're almost certainly facing a very tight player who will only bet on the strongest of cards. Play accordingly if this individual is in the pot.

Help Card _____

Here is a subconscious move that many players make that will cue you on when to fold a marginal hand. After the flop, a quick glance at his or her chip stack is a hint that the player has connected with the board and is planning to make a move.

Shuffling chips is a repetitive behavior associated with nervousness. Watch for _when_ a player shuffles chips. If he's out of a hand, it's not a big deal. If he's in a hand, does he shuffle during every hand, or just occasionally? And, if he shuffles only occasionally, does he tend to win or lose those hands? This is a classic example of the importance of paying attention to a player's behavior, especially when you aren't playing yourself. By doing so, you build your awareness of subtle tells that you can use to your advantage when you are playing a hand.

When betting on marginal cards, watch your opponent as you are betting. If he starts to reach for his chips as you're getting ready to bet, go ahead and complete the bet. This person is holding weak cards and is trying to encourage you to fold by appearing anxious to call or raise.

Similarly, if you are playing on a 3-6 table and you see a player who has prepared 12 chips for a re-raise, it's also a sign of weakness. He's trying to bluff the other bettors. Now, let's say that the two other people still in the hand fold, and this player bets 6. What should you do? Re-raise. If he calls, great; if he re-raises, call the bet and take the next card. All the time, you want to be looking for other tells, to validate your observation that he has a weak hand.

Cards

The way a player treats his cards can provide yet more information about the strength of his hand.

Help Card _____

Keep a close eye on what an opponent does if his wife or girlfriend walks up to the table. If he shows her his hole cards, you can almost guarantee that he has a good hand. Why? Because people want to impress others with the quality of their cards. Obviously, a player wouldn't be in such a hurry to show off a bad hand. The same is true if *any* player shares cards with *any* observer.

Pay attention to how a player treats his hole cards. In Texas Hold'Em, hole cards that are unprotected can be lost if the dealer takes them or if another player's mucked hand falls on them. For this reason, many players will protect their hand with a chip or their fingers. If a player protects his hole cards only *some* of the time, and at other times simply allows them to lie unprotected while the hand is in progress, this is probably a good tell on the strength of his hand. Pay attention to whether he regularly wins hands with protected cards, and if he does, be careful about calling when his chip or hands are on his hole cards.

Bet You Didn't Know

Believe it or not, co-author Andy has seen some blatant tells involving "card protectors." More than once he has played with someone who would look at his cards as soon as he was dealt pre-flop. If the person liked his cards, he'd immediately put his card protector over his cards. If he was going to fold, he wouldn't. You won't find such an obvious tell that often, but sometimes players have similar (although much subtler) tells in how they hold their hole cards.

Some players shuffle their hole cards, but not all the time. This usually indicates impatience before getting to fold a weak hand. After the flop, it may indicate a draw if the player has bet or called. In seven card stud, rapid shuffling before looking at the last card usually indicates a draw.

Bet You Didn't Know

Some players like to look at their cards slowly, first from the side, to see if they can guess what the card is before looking at the index in the corner. That's called squeezing the cards. Some players like to look at their cards one at a time. In both cases, you can often get an idea of their cards by the way they react as they look at them.

The Least You Need to Know

- Chain-smoking can be a sign of a loose player.
- The use of a lucky "comfort item" is more common with weaker players.
- People are sometimes instinctively more protective of stronger hands.

Chapter 9

Online Tells

In This Chapter

- Why some players prefer to play online
- The most common online tells
- Why Auto-Play options are important

Online poker has come a long way in a few short years, and gives dedicated and casual poker players alike the opportunity to play in the comfort and privacy of their own homes. In this chapter, we will discuss the advantages of playing online, playing patterns you need to know, and the most common tells of online players.

Online Poker's Popularity

Online poker has become incredibly popular over the past few years. Millions of people now play poker regularly, thanks in part to the countless number of available sites and ease at which you can find, play and pay for your online poker fun.

Thanks to technology, you can enjoy an exciting game of poker at any time of the day or night, from wherever you happen to be.

Another thing that has made online poker so hot? The stories—which have now become legends—of guys like Chris Moneymaker, regular guys who came from out of nowhere and took the online route to a huge live tournament jackpot.

Co-author Andy is involved with FullTiltPoker. com, so of course that is one online poker site we would definitely recommend. Other popular sites include PokerStars.com and PartyPoker.com

Online Advantages

There are several advantages of playing poker online, especially when it comes to detecting tells of your opponents. In this section, we'll discuss several of the biggest ones.

More Hands Played Per Hour

Because the actual time spent by a live dealer in shuffling and dealing cards is basically eliminated, online games move almost twice as quickly as live games, meaning that you can expect to see about twice as many hands per hour. More hands seen equals more opportunities to outplay your opponents and win their money.

Bet You Didn't Know _____

Hand Histories are a cool feature of online poker sites. Most sites have an option to request or record the action for all of your hands. For example, at Full Tilt Poker, the poker site that co-author Andy Bloch helped design and plays, there's an option to automatically save all hand histories to a directory on the user's machine. The site also has a feature where players can go over the last 50 hands at any table graphically. The hand histories won't help you spot most timing tells, but they will be helpful in tracking player tendencies, which frees you up to take more detailed notes based on time delays. Full Tilt Poker also allows you to take color-coded notes for every opponent.

More Tournaments Available

If you prefer tournament-style play to straight cash games, online poker offers many more opportunities to play this style. You can find tournaments online at almost any time of the day, any day of the week, with many "free-roll" tourneys available to players who log a certain number of hours of play. Compare that to a brick-and-mortar club or casino where tournaments are only held a few times a week at certain hours. Online tournaments are a great way to build your skill in playing this format of poker; many of the recent poker champs began their tournament careers online.

Convenience and Privacy

Depending on where you live, it may take a while to drive to a poker room or casino, put your name on the board for a game, and so on. Once you've gone to all this trouble, obviously you're going to want to stay for a while, making live poker a time-consuming, though very rewarding, experience. Compare this to online poker where you can log on to a site in a matter of minutes, play for half an hour, and log off. For the busy player, this can give you great opportunities to improve your play and hone your skills without spending long hours in a casino. Best of all, as we will discuss later, it gives you the chance to make detailed notes on your opponents, something that would not be allowed in a brick-and-mortar poker room.

The rise of online poker was generally thought to have removed the role of tells from the game of poker. However, serious online players have discovered that is certainly not the case. In fact, it has simplified the use of tells, because there are a lot fewer things to look for (since you can rule out most sights and sounds) and also because, due the fact that online poker is played in the privacy of your own home, you can (and should!) keep detailed records on all your opponents. Depending on which sites you frequent, you can often notice the same players there repeatedly. It helps if you develop a regular schedule, visiting that site at the same days/times repeatedly. That way, you are more likely to encounter the same opponents over and over.

For example, let's say you play on a certain poker site, and you've played several times against an opponent whose screen name is CardShark. You've made note of the fact that every time CardShark showed a long pause followed by a raise, he either won the pot, or had the second-best hand. You are holding a marginal draw hand, and CardShark has just raised after a long pause. What should you do?

A fold is probably the smart move here, since you know from previous observation that this player rarely loses after he has hesitated and decided to raise.

Help Card

Another reason that tells can be such a powerful aid for you in online poker is that fewer players report using them. This means that if you know what to look for when playing online poker, then you have an advantage over the large majority of your opponents.

Auto-Play Patterns

All online poker sites offer certain Auto-Play buttons that the poker player can use to "pre-set" his

desired action before it's actually his turn to play.
The possible Auto-Play options vary from site to
site, but some of the almost-universal options
include the following:

Auto-Post Blinds

This option allows for automatic posting of the big
blind and small blind. It's very common to play
with this enabled, and you can't get much information from this option.

Check/Fold

With this option activated, the player automatically
checks, unless another player has bet ahead of her,
in which case, the hand is folded. If you notice that
a certain player seems to be set in this pattern of
checking or folding, it's probable that she is using
this Auto-Play setting. In this case, what you're
looking for is any case where that player doesn't
check or fold right away; any call or raise indicates
that she has stopped using the Auto-Play and is
actually concentrating on playing her hand. This is
a solid indication that she has a strong hand.

Check/Call Any

With this option activated, the player automatically
checks, unless another player has bet ahead of him,
in which case, he calls the bet. If you notice that a
certain player seems to be set in this pattern of
checking or folding, it's likely that he is using this
Auto-Play setting. In this case, what you're looking

for is any case where that player doesn't check or call right away; any raise indicates that he has stopped using the Auto-Play and is actually concentrating on playing his hand. This is a solid indication that he has a strong hand.

Bet/Raise Any

With this option activated, the player automatically makes the minimum bet, unless another player has bet ahead of him, in which case, the bet is raised. If you notice that a certain player seems to be set in this pattern of betting or raising, it's probable that he is using this Auto-Play setting. In this case, what you're looking for is any case where that player doesn't merely bet the minimum, but raises right away; this is a definite indication that he has stopped using the Auto-Play and is actually concentrating on playing his hand. Now, you're going to have to look at the board and your notes on that player to decide whether he is bluffing or actually playing a strong hand.

Another thing you are looking for is any time that this player simply *calls* a bet. Again, you can tell that he's taken the game off Auto-Play and is actively engaged in the game; you can also deduce that he is probably deliberately slow playing to build the pot for a strong hand. The final deviation to the pattern would be if he simply checked to the next player. In this case, you also know that he is actively playing, and you can expect to see a check-raise, which will confirm your suspicion that he has good hole cards.

| HELP | **Help Card** _____ |

Sometimes players give away information by chatting during a hand. More often, they wait until after the hand to chat, when it will give away information about their mood.

Be a Silent—but Studious—Observer

Some online card rooms allow the player to sit out for a while without losing his or her spot at the table. This is a great way to do a little profiling and make some notes on the opposition before you begin to play. Make notes on the other players at the table. There are only a handful of possible online tells, and a few player types you could be facing.

Determine which players are fish, rocks, and loose aggressives. Figure out who is the strongest player at the table. Now start looking for betting patterns and speed tells to determine the hand strength of your opposition. These observations will put you head and shoulders above the majority of all online players who don't look for tells from their opponents.

Common Online Tells

There are a few common tells that you will notice when playing online. Let's take a look at the most common of these online signals.

Quick Response–Raise

A quick raise off the flop is a good indication that
your opponent has top pair or better. It could also be
an indication that she is using an Auto-Play option of
"Bet/Raise Any." This is where good note-taking will
help you determine if this is simply a loose aggressive
player using the Auto-Play buttons, or if in fact this is
an attentive player who has probably got the top pair.

Quick Response–Call

Frequent quick calls by a player probably indicates
that he is using the "Check/Call Any" Auto-Play
option and that he, and his cards, are probably
weak. Play accordingly.

Quick Response–Check

This player has weak cards and is looking for a free
card. A raise should force him out of the hand,
making way for your cards to play and eliminating
one possible bad beat if the player is allowed to
play cheaply.

Slow Response–Raise

When an online player thinks for a while and then
raises, he almost always has good cards. Read the
board and see what the most dangerous hand would
be. If you're not holding it, this would be a good
time to fold, because your opponent has made his
hand. Just like live poker, the player is trying to
indicate weakness with the long pause, hoping to
make you think that he is pondering whether to

raise or not. In fact, he has a strong hand and is just trying to draw your call. So, disappoint him and fold unless you are in a strong position yourself.

Slow Response–Call

This is a case where a player is actually debating the strength of her hand. Treat a slow call as a bluff, or simply as a case of a weak made hand, like a small pair, and decide how to play your hand accordingly.

> **Bet You Didn't Know**
>
> Keep an eye on the avatars. Full Tilt Poker allows players to select one of several dozen images called "Avatars" to use as their online character. Each avatar has four emotions (Normal, Happy, Angry, and Confused) that the player can switch between at any time, even during hands. If a player is switching his avatar's emotion during a hand, it could be a tell—or it could just mean that he's bored.

The Least You Need to Know

- ◆ Playing poker online can offer you many advantages over playing in-person at a table.
- ◆ Quick or slow responses at certain points in the online action can be revealing tells.
- ◆ When playing poker online, you should have a notebook handy to jot down observations about other players.

Hints and Tricks

In This Chapter

+ Getting opponents to underestimate you
+ Staying unpredictable is key
+ Fold tells can be vital to your own play

We've shown you how to use many different tells to discover an opponent's true hand strength. Now let's conclude by looking at ways to sharpen your skills at spotting tells, using your own "false tells" to deceive your opponents, and making sure that you minimize any unconscious tells that you might be displaying yourself.

Sharpening Your Tell-Spotting Skills

The only way to get good at spotting tells is by practice. There are simply no shortcuts. One way to get started at a table is to sit out a few hands and wait for the big blind to come to you instead of posting up right away. This gives you a chance to observe all the other players for several hands before you actually start to play. Staying focused is another key to making use of tells. If you become bored or tired, your ability to spot key tells will be greatly diminished. If you notice this happening, take a few minutes to stretch your legs, walk to the bar, and refocus yourself.

Another way to practice spotting tells is to make a game of figuring out who the winner will be when you aren't in a hand. How quickly can you predict who is taking the pot? Off the flop? The river? How often can you correctly pinpoint the winner? This exercise will benefit you greatly when you are in a hand.

Help Card

Nowadays, there are lots of ways to sharpen your skills as a poker player. There are tons of books available—you can easily find some at any bookstore or library (see the Resource section at the back of this book for some suggestions). There are even poker training conferences and schools where you can learn from the pros. Do a quick online search to find out if there are any near you.

Tricking Opponents with False Tells

Remember some of the unconscious and "profile" tells that indicated a player who was loose, weak, and relied more on luck than skill? Things like messy chip stacks, flamboyantly waving money to buy chips, drinking heavily at the table?

Well, you can use these things to your advantage, because they're fairly obvious signs of weakness that any experienced player is going to recognize.

Just like you, any other strong player at the table is going to want to play more hands when the other players in the hand are weaker than he or she is. This is because they will be more susceptible to bluffing and will often be playing weaker hands.

Now, if you can get the other strong players to read you as a loose, novice player, then they're going to play a looser game against you than they would if they had correctly read you as the tight, conservative player that you want to be.

But how exactly do you do this?

Well, first, when you sit down, you can wave your money around and attract a little attention by buying chips. Then, you can keep your chip stack pretty loose and messy. You can make an effort to count and stack a little if you are out of a hand, but in general, your little piece of the table should look pretty sloppy. Then you can get out your lucky charm and place it somewhere obvious and handy. You can give it a good rub or a shake every time you win a hand. Oh, and you can order a drink, and sip it slowly. The appearance you are giving is that you are a loose, liquored-up, luck-guided fool. Your opponents should underestimate you, and that gives you a strong initial edge.

Tilt _____

We should warn you: this type of false tell generally won't work if you are playing with your friends or other people who know you very well. They will quickly realize you're not acting like you usually do, and your act will fall flat.

Minimizing Your Own Tells

Of course, you want to minimize your own tells. Wearing dark or reflective glasses should eliminate many eye-related tells. Try to maintain a set style of betting, placing the chips in the pot with the same amount of force every time. Switch up your playing style from time to time. Got strong cards? Act like they're strong, and warn people to get out of the hand. If they don't listen, they'll be sorry when you flash the pocket Aces. Next time, they may think twice when ignoring your warnings. Other times, feign weakness. Practice mastering a "lukewarm" demeanor that you can apply at will.

Often, a strong player will try to talk you into revealing the strength of your hand. He may try to accomplish this by asking about your hand, or describing his hand to you.

Here's an example: Let's say you're heads-up at a 20-40 table with a strong opponent. It's a short table and both other players have folded before the flop. You're holding J-10, and the dealer flops 6-J-10. It is going to be your action, but as soon as the last card on the flop is turned, your opponent starts talking about his hand. "Oh man, I don't think you want to bet this one. I'm one away from a straight ... just kidding, I've only got a pair of Queens ... I mean, 2s ...."

> ### 🃏 Help Card
>
> Occasionally, say once every 10 or 20 hands, take a long shot, like a small pair or a small gutshot straight (a straight filled "inside"), and bet it to the river. You may win, catching your opposition completely by surprise, or you may lose and simply make yourself appear to be a looser player than you really are. In any case, you are unpredictable.

His goal is to get a reaction from you. He want to see whether and how you react to the prospect that he has strong cards, weak cards, or is looking for one more card.

If your opponent notices a reaction from you at the mention of Queens, changing to elation when he changes his story to a pair of 8s, he'll guess that you are holding a marginal pair, something like 9-9, 10-10, J-J ....

On the other hand, if he sees some more blatant sign of strength or weakness from you as he gives his spiel, then it's a good chance that you are "acting" and he can infer that the reverse is true; for example, if you shrug and sigh while he's talking about the possible pairs, he can conclude that you are trying to act as if you are worried by both pairs, and in fact are probably holding strong cards.

How do you prevent an opponent from reading you in the same manner that you are trying to read him? You need to turn the tables and act in the opposite manner expected; strong is strong, weak is weak. If you have marginal cards, you may bluff by acting weak, sighing, shrugging, preparing to fold out of turn.

If the opponent misreads your strength and check, you can get a free card. If not, you may choose to fold. Similarly, with the strong cards from the previous example, you can act strong, by staring down your opponent, or splashing the pot with your chips.

Table of Important Actions

To make things easier, we've compiled a list of actions that convey strength or weakness at the poker table.

If You Want To:	Do This:
Appear Weak	Don't play many hands; frequently fold early
Look Like an Easy Mark	Chat with Friends; dress sloppy; act drunk
Look like a Tight Aggressive	Play selectively; stay cool and collected
Appear Strong down;	Give opponents a stare don't be chatty

Things to Watch Out For

Here are a couple of poker pitfalls—ways that even educated players who have studied the use of tells can get into trouble. We'd like to mention these, so that you can make sure not to make these mistakes yourself. The first one may seem *too* obvious, but you'd be surprised how often it happens!

Keep Your Secrets!

Once you've discovered an opponent's tell, you want to be very careful not to show that you've picked up on it. Some people, believe it or not, will actually come right out and say things like "I knew you were bluffing because I saw you glance at your hole cards …."

It happens. Maybe those folks think that they're intimidating their opponent or throwing them off their game. Maybe it's a quick ego boost. Whatever the reason, all it does is let everyone at the table know that you're watching them, and cause them to tighten up and hide any of their own tells, while causing the target of your remark to correct herself, costing you the opportunity to profit from that particular tell in the future.

Even worse, she may pull the old switcheroo and turn the tell around and use it to sucker you into betting. In this example, she may have just made a hand of three Aces, but peeks at the hole cards, causing you to play her as if she were bluffing, costing you substantially.

Don't Ignore Fold Tells

One common mistake made by players who have learned the basics of using tells is to only look for tells indicating for them to call or raise. In fact, almost twice as many tells indicate that folding is the best option. However, your natural aggressive instinct is to raise and call; after all, that's how you win hands, right? In fact, you make more money in the long run by *saving* money on all those bad hands that you fold early.

Summary

Well, we've pretty much covered all the important aspects of the art of poker tells. By starting out with the basic theory of tells and the science behind body language, you've built a good foundation for taking advantage of the power of tells. Next, we illustrated how to pick out the novice players at the table and use that knowledge to help you choose the best hands to play—pots where many weak players and few strong ones are going for the money.

The ability to quickly and accurately place opponents in one of the major player types was the next step—again, enabling you to make basic decisions on what pots to play for and how to treat individual players in heads-up play. We looked at the differences between blatant and subtle tells, and discussed what to look for when playing against other strong poker players. A deeper look at body language, sounds, and tells involving props like chips or drinks finished out the brick-and-mortar tells. Our final analysis was of the common online poker tells and how to interpret them. In this last chapter, we looked at some ways to deceive the opposition about your own level of play and playing style, and how to mask some basic tells of your own. And we discussed some of the most common mistakes players make in revealing tells, or only looking for tells that indicate a call or raise.

Now, there's nothing left to do but go to the poker table and put your newfound knowledge to work for you. Good luck!

The Least You Need to Know

- The best way to become a tell-spotting pro is through lots of practice and careful observation.

- If you have good acting skills (and a bit of luck) you can sometimes fool opponents into thinking you're a weaker player.

- It's important to be very careful not to give off tells of your own.

- When you spot other players' tells, keep them to yourself. Don't announce this discovery to the rest of the table.

Appendix A

Poker Glossary

ace magnets   A slang term meaning a pair of Kings.

all-in   A play in which the player bets all his or her remaining chips.

ante   A small amount of a bet, contributed by each player to fund the pot at the start of a poker hand.

bad beat   A situation in which a hand would be considered an underdog ends up beating a seemingly better hand.

bankroll   The amount of money you personally have available to bet.

blind   A forced bet from one or more players before cards are dealt.

blind raise   To raise without first looking at your cards.

bluff   To act like you have a better hand than you actually do.

board   Common cards in a community game that are placed on the board.

busted   To be broke; out of chips or money.

button   Player deemed to be in the dealer position. Often indicated by a flat disk, called the dealer button.

buy-in   The amount you must pay to participate in a tournament; it's similar to an entrance fee.

card room   The room or section of a casino (or other establishment) where card games are being held.

cashing in   Usually done when you are finished playing, this is the process of trading in your chips for money. Also known as "cashing out."

check   Passing without betting. Essentially, betting an amount of zero dollars.

community cards   The common cards that can be used by any player in a community card game.

cowboy   A slang term used to refer to a king.

deal   To pass out cards to each player, or place cards on the board.

deck   A complete set of cards. Generally, 52 cards except in cases where the joker is used.

Dolly Parton   A slang term meaning a two-card hand consisting of a 9 and a 5.

draw   To replace cards in a hand.

face card   A card featuring a "picture" instead of a number: jack, queen or king.

fish   A player with poor poker skills.

fish hooks   A slang term used to refer to jacks.

five and dime   A slang term used to refer to a two-card combination consisting of a 5 and a 10.

flop   The first three community cards placed on the board in Texas Hold'Em.

fold   To give up your cards.

four of a kind   Four cards of the same rank. Also sometimes called "quads."

four horsemen   A slang term meaning a four-card hand consisting of all Kings. Also sometimes known as a "posse."

full house   A hand consisting of three cards of one suit, plus two cards from a second suit.

flush   Five cards that are all of the same suit.

foul   A hand considered invalid for some reason. Also known as a "dead hand."

full house   A hand made up of a pair and three of a kind.

gutshot straight   A straight filled "inside."

Hilton sisters   A slang term meaning two Queens.

hole   The concealed card(s).

house   The casino or other establishment which is hosting the game.

hot If a player is on a lucky streak, they are said to be "hot." Likewise, a player who hasn't been winning is said to be "cold."

maniac An extremely aggressive player.

muck To discard a hand.

nuts A term used to represent the best possible hand.

pair Two cards with the same rank.

pocket cards Your individual cards, visible to you alone.

pocket pair In hold 'em, a starting hand with a pair.

position The location of a player in relation to the blind or button.

protecting your hand Keeping your hands or chips on your cards, to keep it from being inadvertently fouled or mucked by the dealer.

rack The tray in which chips are stored or transported.

rags (or ragged) Cards that don't appear to help anyone; useless cards.

raise To increase the amount of the previous bet.

rank The numerical value of a card. Cards have two important characteristics: rank and suit.

river The last community card placed on the board in Texas Hold'Em.

rock   Someone who plays very tight and raises with caution, only when he has the best hands.

royal flush   A hand consisting of the 10 through ace cards, all of a single suit. This is considered the best hand in poker.

satellite   A type of poker tournament in which the prize isn't cash, but admittance to a bigger, higher-stakes tournament.

short stack   A pile of chips which is smaller than those of other players at the table.

showdown   The conclusion of the hand, where the remaining players show their cards to determine who has the best hand.

Shuffle   To mix the cards in a deck prior to play. When done by an experienced dealer, this can be an impressive sight.

side pot   Also known as a side bet, this is a separate, additional pot formed when at least one player is all in.

splashing the pot   Throwing chips at the pot instead of keeping them in an organized stack. This is considered rude behavior at the poker table.

straight   Five cards in numerical order.

straight flush   Five cards in numerical order, all of the same suit.

suited   Cards that are of the same suit.

tell   A clue or hint a player unknowingly exhibits that tells others what kind of hand he or she has.

three of a kind   Three cards with the same numerical value, such as three 8's. Also known as "trips."

tilt   To play in reckless or thoughtless way.

trips   *See* three of a kind.

turn   The fourth community card. Also called "fourth street."

under the gun   Player in the position that must bet first in a round.

underdog   A player or hand that does not seem to have a very good chance of winning.

wheel   A straight comprised of cards in sequential order from ace through five.

Rules of Poker Etiquette

Although we're including this for poker-playing purposes, most of these rules are actually good guidelines for many other daily activities and games, as well.

- **Don't be offensive.** Unless you're playing in a barroom with your old college buddies, avoid telling dirty jokes and using foul language.

- **Don't be a sore loser.** No matter how much money you've lost, don't take it out on your opponents, the dealer, or innocent bystanders.

- **Don't be a sore winner, either.** If you're lucky enough to win, it's okay to smile and look happy. It's not okay to jump up and down, act like a jerk, or demean other players with taunts such as, "Who's the poker champ now, loser?"

- **Treat the cards with care.** Just as you shouldn't abuse the dealer or other players, there's no need to mistreat the cards, either. It's not the cards' fault that you may not have a great hand. Tearing, bending, or otherwise damaging cards is something you should never do.

- **Stay clean and relatively sober.** Becoming an obnoxious drunk or being under the influence of illegal substances won't make you the kind of player others want at their table.

- **Don't splash your chips.** Splashing chips into the pot is a no-no.

- **Don't take forever.** In football, they call it a "delay of game." In poker, it's stalling the action. Either way, it's not a good thing.

- **Avoid revealing your cards at the wrong time.** If you are folding, you should hand in your cards face down. Otherwise, you will reveal not only your cards but also important information that can affect the outcome of the game.

A Poker Primer

The Basics

Before you go anywhere near a poker table, you need to know how to play. That's going to make things much easier. If you already understand the basics and the how-to of poker, then you can probably skip this section.

All poker games played in casinos and card rooms today involve a five-card hand. This means that the best hand will always consist of the best possible five cards no matter what game you are playing. Poker is played with a standard 52-card deck. For Draw poker and Lowball, a joker or "bug" is sometimes added to the deck. The 52 cards are divided into four suits: Spades, Hearts, Diamonds, and Clubs. Each suit contains cards that rank 2 through King, and an Ace, which can be used as either the high or the low card.

Hand Rankings

Even in games where more than five cards are used, such as Omaha and Hold'Em, the best possible hand always refers to a five-card hand. It is important to know the best hands before you begin playing any kind of poker.

The best possible hand in poker is the **royal flush**. *(Note: If wild cards are used in a home game, then five of a kind would top a royal flush as the best hand.)* A royal flush is a straight flush consisting of the top five cards in the deck, A, K, Q, J, 10, all of the same suit. As you can guess, there are only four ways to make a Royal Flush.

The next best possible hand is a **straight flush**. A straight flush is five cards all of the same suit, all in sequential order, such as 6, 7, 8, 9, 10, all spades.

After a straight flush comes **four of a kind**. This is four of the same card such as Js, Jc, Jd, Jh. The fifth card in this hand would be your next best card, known as your "kicker."

After four of a kind, the next best hand is a **full house**. A full house is sometimes known as a boat or full boat. A full house consists of three of one card and two of another card, such as 8s, 8h, 8c, 4d, 4c. A full house can contain any three of one card and any two of another card. When announcing how high your full house is, it is common to announce your hand by declaring your three-of-a-kind card and then your two-of-a-kind card. For instance, the above hand would be declared as "eights full of fours."

A **flush** is the next best hand after a full house. A flush is five cards all of the same suit such as Kh, 9h, 7h, 4h, 3h. A flush is only as good as the highest-ranked card in the flush. When two people both have a flush, the person with the highest single card in that flush will be the winner. The above hand would be declared as a "king high flush." That king high flush could be beat by someone with an "ace high flush." If two players both have a king high flush, then the next biggest card in the flush would determine the winner. If the next biggest card in the flush is the same in both hands, then the third biggest card in the flush would determine the winner, and so on, down to the fifth biggest card in the flush. If both players have equally ranked cards in the flush, then they would split the pot. Suits never matter in determining the best hand; all four suits are equal in value.

The next best hand is a **straight.** This is just simply five cards all in numerical order of different suits, such as Js, 10h, 9s, 8c, 7h. (Remember, if they are all of the same suit, it would be a straight flush.) This hand would be declared a "jack high straight." It would beat a "ten high straight," and it would be beaten by a "queen high straight" (Qh, Js, 10d, 9h, 8c).

After a straight comes **three of a kind**, known as "trips." Three of a kind is three cards of the same numerical value, along with your next two biggest cards, or kickers, such as 9s, 9h, 9c, As, Jd. In community card games, those in which players share some of the cards, it is possible for more than one player to have the same three of a kind. In this case, the person with the best kicker would win the pot. If both players had the same first kicker, then the second kicker would come into play.

The next best hand is **two pair**. This is simply two separate pairs such as 10s, 10h, 8c, 8h, and then your next best card as the kicker. When two or more players both have two pair, the player with the highest pair wins the hand. The ranking of the second pair only matters if the highest pair in each player's hand is the same. As, Ah, 4c, 4d would beat Ks, Kc, Jh, Jc; however, it would be beat by Ac, Ad, 7s, 7c, because the second pair would come into effect after the top pair in each hand tied. (If two players have the same two pair, then their next highest-ranked card would determine the winner.)

One pair is the next best hand and consists of just two cards of equal numerical value, along with the player's three best-ranked cards as kickers. The same rules for determining the winner apply.

If you are playing with a really unlucky group and no player has so much as a pair, then the winner of the pot would be determined by high card. The player's best five cards would be their hand, for example, As, Jh, 9c, 7h, 4d would be known as "ace-jack high." In determining the winner, the highest-ranked card would win the pot, followed by the next highest card, and so on, down to the fifth card if needed. To put it simply, the rarer the hand, the more valuable it is.

Games

This section reviews some of the most-common poker games.

Draw Games

Draw games involve card exchanges between players. Players first receive five cards face down. If they decide to remain in the game, they must bet or call, if that is the play being made. Players then have the option to exchange a number of cards, ranging from none to the maximum amount of cards that a player is initially dealt. The exchange is done with the remaining deck of cards that is handled by the dealer. This exchange with the dealer is referred to as "the draw." Once the draw is complete, and depending upon which game is being played, this exchange can occur once or twice or whatever is deemed as so by each respective game.

The most recurring draw game is a five-card draw, in which each player is dealt five cards. After looking at her cards, she can decide to exchange as many cards as she wishes (up to five cards in a five-card draw.) The number of times that players are allowed to exchange is solely determined by the dealer's specification.

In regard to draw games, betting occurs after players have "drawn" or exchanged their cards.

Tactically speaking, it is useful to take note of how many cards players choose to exchange. For example, if a player decides to keep all her original cards, there is a good possibility that she has a good standing hand. Whereas, if a player chooses to exchange all her cards, there is great possibility that she has a no working hand.

An obvious difference between draw games is the number of times draws are allowed. Additionally, some draw games include differences in what is/are wild cards.

Stud Games

Ultimately the most obvious and simplistic difference between stud and draw games is that in stud games, cards are revealed to others, whether they are particular to each individual or used as communal cards. Simply put, stud games are those in which the first round of cards and/or the last round of cards is dealt face down, while the others are dealt face up, exposed to all. Stud games can consist of games in which players receive cards at the initial deal, and they end up obtaining more cards during the succession of the game, or they can include games in which players initially receive all their cards, but show them as time progresses.

An example of a stud game is seven-card stud. Initially, two cards are dealt face down and one card up to each player. The player who has the low card begins betting; each player, subsequently, must call or check (no action), raise, or fold (not remain in the game). After each player is dealt another three cards, face up, another round of betting follows. Finally, a last card is dealt face down, and subsequently they go through another round of betting. The player with the highest poker hand wins.

Seven-card stud can be played in a high or low split. The sole difference lies in that the high split requires the player with the highest card to begin betting.

Texas Hold'Em

In this game, each player is dealt two cards face down. Before cards are even dealt, two players to the left of the dealer button must automatically place small and large bets (in amounts relevant to each game). After the initial two cards are dealt and looked at by the players, they begin a round of betting. Subsequently, three cards are dealt face up that are communal cards—in other words, every player can use these cards to add to his or her individual cards. These three cards are called the flop. Another round of betting follows after the flop is revealed. The dealer then burns a card and reveals another card. This card is called the turn card. Again, another round of betting follows after the turn card. Then the dealer burns another card and reveals the last card—this is called the river. After the last card is dealt, players can use any of the five communal cards and/or their individual two cards to form the best poker hand they can. When the last round of betting has finished, the players begin to reveal their hands—this is referred to as the showdown. The best hand wins—or if there are any ties, then the players split the pot. There are other variations of Texas Hold'Em; however this method of the game is one that has become very popular to the public.

Omaha

Though Omaha may seem similar to Texas Hold'Em, it has its differences. Initially, as is in Texas Hold'Em, players to the left of the dealer must put in blinds. Consequently, each player will receive four cards face down, followed by a round of betting. Communal cards are dealt face up in the same way that occurs in Texas Hold'Em. After the last round of betting, players expose their hands. If there is a qualifying low hand, that player splits the pot with the winning high hand. In order to qualify for a low hand, the player must have five cards of 8 or lower (with no pair), using two from his individual hand and three from the communal cards. If there are no qualifying low hands, the player with the typical highest poker hand takes the pot. Therefore, although the type of betting that occurs is similar to Texas Hold'Em, the initial drop is different as well as the factors that qualify the winning high (or low) hands.

Limit vs. No-Limit vs. Pot Limit

In limit poker, the bet is as it seems: "limited," or "set." For instance, if the limit to a game were $4 to $6, all bets and raises would be $4 in the first couple of rounds and $6 in the last couple of rounds. In no-limit poker, a player can choose how much to bet—thereby making the amount one chooses to bet an important factor. No-limit poker involves the most strategy as well as the most wins, since there are no boundaries. For this reason, it is regarded as the most exciting type of poker. In pot-limit poker, the maximum amount to bet is the size of the pot. However, it is essential to keep in mind that if a player were to re-raise, that additional amount is added to the initial pot size.

Limit

In limit Hold'Em, the betting is structured and cannot be adjusted. If you are playing $15 to $30, the bets before the flop and on the flop are always $15. The bets on the turn and on the river are always $30. In addition to the initial bet, you would be able to make raises of the same amount as the initial bet on each betting street. Depending on where you are playing, you are allowed either three or four raises. In some places, if only two people are involved in the pot, then you can make unlimited raises. It is a rare occasion, though, that two players will raise each other beyond three or four raises; and if they do, then it usually means they both have the same hand. Only a foolish person would continue to raise beyond four times without the best possible hand.

Pot Limit

Pot limit differs from limit in that instead of a structured bet, you are allowed to bet as little as the big blind, up to the total amount of money in the pot. If you are playing in a $5 to $10 pot-limit game and you are the first person to act, then you are allowed to bet the minimum of $10, or you can raise the size of the pot. In pot limit, when figuring out the size of the pot, the amount that you have to call is figured into that bet. In the above example, if you wanted to raise the size of the pot, you could call $10 and then raise $25 more for a total bet of $35. In many places, the small blind counts as a full bet when determining the size of the pot, and you would then be able to make a total bet of $40. The next person to act then has the choice of folding, calling $40, or raising any amount between the amount of your raise ($30), and the size of the pot—in this case $100, for a total bet of $140. (They call the $40 bet and then raise the size of the pot, small blind of $10, big blind of $10, your bet of $40, and their own called bet of $40, for a total of $140.) As you can see, this can add up quickly and it makes the game much larger than an inexperienced player may realize. In the above situation, if everybody folded back around to you and you called the $100 raise, then the pot size would be $300 ($5 small blind counted as $10, $10 big blind, $140 from you, plus $140 from your opponent). After the flop, your betting choices would be any amount from $10 to the size of the pot, or $300. If you were to bet $300, your opponent could, if she chose, raise $900, making it a total of $1200 (the $300 she would call, your $300 bet, plus the $300 already in the pot). This type of raising is not unusual in pot-limit games; it happens quite frequently, and oftentimes both players will get all of their money into the pot before the turn card is ever seen.

No limit

No limit is very simple to understand. Like its name suggests, there is no limit to the amount you can bet other than what you have in front of you. At any time you can bet anywhere from the amount of the big blind, up to the total amount that you have in play in front of you. This ability to make big bets in pot-limit and no-limit games has made them known as big-bet poker when compared to limit games.

Appendix D

Resources

This appendix contains additional resources to help you find your way in the world of poker.

Websites

AndyBloch.com. Co-author Andy's website.

AnnieDuke.com. Personal website of poker pro Annie Duke.

ChrisFerguson.com. Personal website of poker champ Chris "Jesus" Ferguson.

ClonieGowen.com. Personal website of professional poker player Clonie Gowen.

ChrisMoneymaker.com. Personal website of poker champ Chris Moneymaker.

FossilmanPoker.com. Personal website of poker champ Greg "Fossilman" Raymer.

FullTiltPoker.com. Play poker against co-author Andy and other top players.

PokerWire.com. Up-to-the-minute detailed coverage of major poker tournaments.

UltimatePokerChallenge.com. Official website of the Ultimate Poker Challenge.

WorldPokerTour.com. Official site of the World Poker Tour. Check out player profiles, event schedules, and more.

www.WPTfan.com. The Unoffocial World Poker Tour fan site, run by co-author Andy.

WSOP.com. Official website of the World Series of Poker

Books

Bringing Down the House, The Inside Story of Six M.I.T. Students Who Took Vegas for Millions by Ben Mezrich—Co-author Andy is featured in this exciting book.

The Complete Idiot's Guide to Gambling Like a Pro, Fourth Edition by Stanford Wong and Susan Spector—Everything you need to know about winning at casino gambling.

Fundamentals of Poker by Mason Malmuth and Lynne Loomis—A good guide for beginners, covering the basics of all popular versions of poker.

Hold 'em for the Advanced Player and *Theory of Poker,* both by David Sklansky.

Index

Q

R

Learn how to deal with Texas Hold'em!

- The stakes and strategies of the three types of betting
- A revealing look at the mistakes most beginners make
- Fun quizzes to help you hone your card-playing skills

THE POCKET IDIOT'S GUIDE TO

Texas Hold'em

- **Idiot-proof explanations** of the rules of the game
- **Simple tips** on evaluating cards and your opponents
- **Winning strategies** and tactics for pulling in the chips

Randy Burgess and
Carl Baldassarre

1-59257-32
$9.95

Available at your favorite bookseller and online retailer everywhere!

www.idiotsguides.com

ALPH